I0014216

IfColog Proceedings

Volume 1

Proceedings of URC* 2010

Undergraduate Research in Computer Science – Theory and Applications

Student Conference

Volume 1
Proceedings of URC* 2010. Undergraduate Research in Computer Science
– Theory and Applications. Student Conference
Maribel Fernández and Kathleen Steinhöfel, eds.

The International Federation for Computational Logic has been created and legally registered as a charity in London. IFCoLog's members are the current (and future) communities related to computational logic.

The IFCoLog Proceedings Series is a non-profit series designed to simplify the process of publishing proceedings of conferences and workshops. The series is dedicated to encouraging greater interaction of academics and students at all levels.

Proceedings of URC* 2010
Undergraduate Research in Computer Science – Theory and Applications
Student Conference

Edited by

Maribel Fernández

and

Kathleen Steinhöfel

ISBN 978-1-84890-026-4

College Publications
Scientific Director: Dov Gabbay
Managing Director: Jane Spurr
Department of Computer Science
King's College London, Strand, London WC2R 2LS, UK

http://www.collegepublications.co.uk

Original cover design by Laraine Welch
Printed by Lightning Source, Milton Keynes, UK

Contents

Preface

The URC* (Undergraduate Research in Computer Science - Theory and Applications) conference aims at promoting research in computer science and interdisciplinary topics amongts undergraduate students. The conference provides a forum that brings together undergraduate students, postgraduate students and leading scientists. By introducing students to new research results and techniques it encourages them to start conducting research and producing research results already during their undergraduate studies.

The first URC* conference took place at King's College London, 24-26 March 2010, in association with a Spring School on Information and Software Security.

The programme of the conference included eight student contributions as well as invited talks by Maxime Crochemore, Anthony Finkelstein, Chris Hankin, Ian Mackie, Willard McCarty, Raja Nagarajan, Mark Ryan and Alexander Tiskin.

This volume contains selected papers presented by students at the conference, covering a wide range of topics, including algorithm design (in particular, the design of heuristic algorithms for the maximum-leaf spanning tree problem, and the analysis of speed scaling algorithms), programming language design (in particular, language based security, the use of effect systems for automating model extraction, and results on adaptation languages using visual environments) and applications to ray tracing optical phenomena and pattern matching in MIDI files.

The Programme Committee of URC* 2010 consisted of:

- Andreas Albrecht (Queen's University Belfast)
- Roy Crole (University of Leicester)
- Artur Czumaj (University of Warwick)
- Thomas Erlebach (University of Leicester)
- Maribel Fernández (King's College London), co-chair
- Anthony Finkelstein (University College London)
- Marcelo Fiore (University of Cambridge)
- Leszek Gasieniec (University of Liverpool)
- Gregory Gutin (Royal Holloway)
- Costas Iliopoulos (King's College London)
- Jens Krinke (King's College London)
- Mark Lee (University of Birmingham)
- Richard Overill (King's College London)
- Detlef Plump (University of York)
- Tomasz Radzik (King's College London)
- Kathleen Steinhöfel (King's College London), co-chair
- Iain Stewart (University of Durham)

The conference was sponsored by the Department of Computer Science at King's College London, and was part of the King's-Warwick project, funded by HFCE, which aims to nurture a passion for learning and research amongst students, through an active and outward-looking curriculum.

vii

We would like to thank all those who contributed to URC* 2010. Special thanks to the invited speakers, the Programme Committee members and the external reviewers, for their support and efficient work. We also thank our colleagues in the Department of Computer Science, who encouraged students to participate in the conference and advised them in their research projects. We are grateful to Elliot Fairweather, Leonidas Kapsokalivas, Olivier Namet, and Matthew Shaw (PhD students in the Department of Computer Science), and to Kelly Androutsopoulos and David Clark (the organisers of the Spring School on Information and Software Security) for their help with the local organisation.

Maribel Fernández and Kathleen Steinhöfel

London, July 2010

Development and Experimental Comparison of Exact and Heuristic Algorithms for the Maximum-Leaf Spanning Tree Problem

Christian Brüggemann,* Tomasz Radzik

Department of Computer Science, King's College London

Abstract

Given a connected, undirected and unweighted graph G, the maximum leaf spanning tree problem (MLSTP) is to find the spanning tree of G, that has the maximum number of leaves. In this report, we present experimental evaluation of the performance of exact algorithms for this problem and several heuristic solutions. The heuristic which we propose is a constructive heuristic. We evaluate the algorithm by experiments and compare results to existing exact and heuristic algorithms.

1   Introduction

Given a connected, undirected and unweighted graph G, we consider the maximum leaf spanning tree problem (MLSTP) as to find a spanning tree of G with a maximum number of leaves. The MLSTP is known to be NP-complete [4] and MAX SNP-complete [5]. Finding the maximum leaf spanning tree of a graph has many applications, for instance in circuit layouts [6]. In this report, we present an experimental evaluation of the performance of exact and heuristic algorithms for this problem. For our experimental evaluations, we apply the algorithms on random graphs as well as complete grid graphs in order to be able to compare our results with those of [1]. In addition to that, we also use incomplete grid graphs. The purpose of this report is to discuss the MLSTP from different point of views (exact algorithms and heuristic solutions).

This report is structured in the following way: In Section 2, we describe an exact algorithm for the MLSTP proposed by Fujie [1] and discuss possible changes to this algorithm. Section 3 describes the test instances we generated for our simulations and in Section 4, we present the results obtained from exact algorithms for the MLSTP. We propose a new heuristic approach called Priority-BFS in Section 5 and compare its

---

*Supported by EPSRC Vacation Bursary Scheme for undergraduate students

performance with other known heuristics. Finally, in Section 6, we present and discuss the test results obtained from all algorithms.

The Priority-BFS heuristic, which we propose in Section 5, improves on previous constructive heuristics for grid graphs and also gives very good results for random graphs and d-regular graphs. We suspect that the Priority-BFS algorithm can be further improved and more importantly we believe that it can be used in the context of exact algorithms to improve their running time.

2   Exact algorithms for the MLSTP

Fujie [1] proposed an exact algorithm for the MLSTP, which is based on the Branch-and-Bound approach and incorporates a very efficient heuristic for selecting subproblems for expansion. A subproblem is denoted as (S_1, S_0, F), where (S_1, S_0, F) is a partition of V. S_1 is the set of vertices that all have to be leaves. S_0 is the set of vertices that all have to be non-leaves and F is the set of the remaining vertices. A vertex in F can either be a leaf or a non-leaf. Fujie [1] shows that the solution to the following problem (P1) is an upper bound on the number of leaves in any spanning tree extending (S_1, S_0, F).

(P1)

$$\text{maximize} \quad \sum_{i \in F} \frac{|\delta(i)|}{|\delta(i)| - 1} - \sum_{e \in E} d_e x_e + |S_1|$$

subject to

$$x \in ST_G,$$
$$x(\delta(i)) \leq 1 \quad (i \in S_1),$$

where

$$d_e = \begin{cases} \frac{1}{|\delta(i)| - 1} + \frac{1}{|\delta(j)| - 1}, & \text{for } e = \{i, j\} \text{ with } i, j \in F \\ \frac{1}{|\delta(i)| - 1}, & \text{for } e = \{i, j\} \text{ with } i \in F, j \notin F \\ 0, & \text{otherwise.} \end{cases}$$

$\delta(i)$ is the set of edges adjacent to vertex i

$x = (x_e | e \in E)$ is a vector of edges and $x(\delta(i)) = \displaystyle\sum_{e \in \delta(i)} x_e$ for $i \in V$

ST_G is the set of all spanning trees of G

The initial configuration of the algorithm is $(\emptyset, \emptyset, V)$. The generated configurations are kept on a stack S. Therefore the subproblem selection corresponds to a depth-first search. The branch and bound algorithm works as follows.

1. **(Initialization)** Run three different heuristics:

   - A breadth first search algorithm rooted at every vertex $v \in V$ of the input graph G.

2

- The 3-approximation algorithm of Lu and Ravi [2].
- The 2-approximation algorithm of Solis-Oba [3].

Let LB be the number of leaves of the best solution of the three algorithms. If $LB = |V| - 1$ then stop. (In that case, the solution obtained is already optimal). Otherwise, push the initial configuration $(\emptyset, \emptyset, V)$ onto the stack S.

2. **(Subproblem selection)** If $S = \emptyset$ then stop. Otherwise, pop (S_1, S_0, F) from S. If $|S_1| + |F| \leq LB$ then go to 2 (no spanning tree consistent with this partial solution can improve LB).

3. **(Checking feasibility)** Check whether there exists a spanning tree of G, where each node in S_1 is a leaf. If not, go to 2. (Remark: One could also check here whether there is a spanning tree such that the set of leaves contains S_1 and the set of non-leaves contains S_0. The latter condition is more difficult to check, but might give a better performance.)

4. **(Updating a lower bound)** If $S_1 > LB$ then, for $v \in S_0 \cup F$, run the breadth first search algorithm rooted at v in the graph $G \backslash S_1$, to make a spanning tree in T in G, of which S_1 is a subset of leaves. Let LB be the number of leaves in T - the improved solution value.

5. **(Upper bounding)** Solve Problem (P1) to compute an upper bound UB on the number of leaves in any spanning tree extending this partial solution (S_1, S_0, F). If $\lfloor UB \rfloor \leq LB$, go to 2 ($\lfloor UB \rfloor$ is the greatest integer not greater than UB).

6. **(Subproblem selection)** Choose $v = argmax\{|\delta_G(u)| : u \in F\}$. Push (G, S_1', S_0, F') followed by (G, S_1, S_0', F') on the stack S, where $S_1' = S_1 \cup v$, $S_0' = S_0 \cup v$ and $F' = F \backslash v$. Go to 2.

In step 5 of the Fujie algorithm, solving Problem (P1) can be done by a standard minimum spanning tree computation in graph $G \backslash S_1$ with edge costs d_e, and then, for $i \in S_1$, connecting i and a vertex $j \in V \backslash S_1$ with the minimum cost $d_{\{i,j\}}$. In step 6 the next subproblem to be considered is the subproblem in which the vertex $v \in F$ with maximum degree is considered as the next element of S_0. This generally is a good heuristic especially for dense graphs. However, when it comes to sparse graphs or grid graphs (especially incomplete grid graphs), this heuristic does not perform well. This is due to the fact that for grid graphs and sparse graphs the degree of most vertices is low. Therefore the heuristic selects more or less arbitrary vertices and the search tree becomes big.

The Fujie algorithm selects the next partial configuration in depth-first order in the search tree of the partial solutions. We investigate whether this can be improved by keeping the generated partial configurations in a priority queue and selecting the one with the highest upper bound. We denote this algorithm as "PQ-Fujie". The PQ-Fujie algorithm has a similar structure to the Fujie algorithm. Instead of a stack S we use a priority queue Q. In step 2, we extract the element with the maximum key from Q, where the key is the upper bound of this subproblem. In step 6, when the two subproblems are generated, we check if they are feasible and calculate their upper

3

bounds (as in step 5 of the Fujie algorithm). Therefore, steps 3 and 5 can be omitted in the PQ-Fujie algorithm.

3   Test graphs

In our experiments we use the following types of graphs. Random graphs and grid graphs were also used in the previous study [1], so we can compare our results with those from [1].

Random graphs. We generate a random graph using two input parameters n and p, where n is the number of vertices in the graph and p is the density of the graph. More precisely, p is the probability of two vertices forming an edge in the graph. If a generated graph is disconnected, we dismiss this graph and generate a new one until we obtain a connected graph.

Random d-regular graphs. We decided to also run experiments on d-regular graphs, that is graphs such that all vertices have degree d. Generating such graphs can be done in the following way. Take d copies of each vertex to create a sequence of vertices of length $n * d$. Randomly permute this sequence. For each node at an odd position in this permuted sequence, put an edge between this node and the next node in the permuted sequence. If the neighbour of a vertex is the same vertex in the graph, we dismiss the graph and generate a new one.

Complete grid graphs. Because random graphs are not very likely to occur in applications of the MLSTP, we decided to focus our evaluation of heuristic and meta-heuristic solutions on grid graphs. Let n denote the number of rows in the grid and m the number of columns. Therefore the number of vertices in the graph is $n * m$. The value (1) given below is the lower bound on the maximum number of leaves in a spanning tree of the grid graph, assuming $n \geq m$; see the construction of spanning trees in grid graphs given in [1].

$$mn - 2n - (m - 4) - \left\lfloor \frac{m - 4}{3} \right\rfloor (n - 2). \tag{1}$$

It is also shown in [1] that the upper bound on the number of leaves is

$$\frac{2}{3}mn. \tag{2}$$

The lower and upper bounds given in (1) and (2) are relatively close. Suppose that $m = 3k + 1$ for some $k \geq 1$. Then the upper bound is equal to $2kn + \frac{2}{3}n$, while the lower bound is equal to $2kn - k + 1$. Therefore, the difference between the lower and upper bounds is only $O(n)$.

4

Incomplete grid graphs. Grid graphs are interesting because they turn out to be significantly harder instances for MLSTP algorithms than random graphs. However, very good constructive solutions for grid graphs are known (see the bounds (1) and (2) and the construction given in [1]), and heuristic approaches have problems reaching even the lower bound. Moreover, we would not be very surprised if someone came up with a construction of a spanning tree of a grid with the maximum possible number of leaves. This motivates experiments with incomplete grid graphs. An incomplete grid graph is a graph with n rows and m columns, that has k edges missing. We generate such graphs by removing k random edges from an $n * m$ grid graph. If the graph becomes disconnected, we dismiss it and run the same process again until we obtain a graph that is connected. Incomplete grid graphs may actually reflect better inputs in some applications of the MLSTP than complete grid graphs.

4   Results of exact algorithms for the MLSTP

Tables 2, 3 and 4 compare the performance of the Fujie and PQ-Fujie algorithms. In these tables, the first two columns specify the graphs, columns BFS, PBFS and maxPBFS show the result obtained from those three heuristic approaches (this is discussed later in Section 5) and column opt gives the number of leaves for the maximum leaf spanning tree. Columns Fujie and PQ-Fujie show the performance of our implementations of these algorithms. Column problems shows the number of generated subproblems, until the optimal solution is found, while column time shows the time it took the algorithm to compute the optimum value in seconds. The lower values are shown in bold. Both algorithms have been tested on the same graphs. Each experiment has been done 20 times and the average values are given in the tables.

It turns out that for random graphs the Fujie algorithm which uses a priority queue (algorithm PQ-Fujie) gives better results only if the graph is relatively sparse (see Table 2). For dense graphs the heuristic of selecting nodes with many edges as interior nodes seems to be a much better mechanism than using a priority queue. Table 3 shows, that the Fujie algorithm is about 3 times faster than the PQ-Fujie algorithm on d-regular graphs. However, we could only evaluate a very limited number of experiments, since the computation on larger graphs was not feasible.

Table 4 shows that the implementation using a priority queue clearly outperforms the original Fujie algorithm on grid graphs with randomly removed edges. As mentioned earlier, this might be due to the fact that many vertices in set F have the same degree.

5 Constructive heuristics for the MLSTP

The Breadth-First-Search traversal of graph G gives relatively good solutions to the MLSTP for random graphs and random d-regular graphs. However, for grid graphs it gives very poor solutions, as can be seen in Table 1. For instance on a $20*40$ complete grid graph the breadth first search gives a tree with only 80 leaves, although the lower bound (1) is 514. The approximation algorithm proposed by Lu and Ravi [2] as well as the approximation algorithm proposed by Solis-Oba [3] both offer a significant improvement compared to the solution obtained from BFS on grid graphs.

We would like to have even better constructive heuristics to be able to compute fast good solutions. Such heuristics could be used within an exact algorithm to provide good initial lower bounds. More importantly, we need good constructive heuristics to compute starting configurations for meta heuristics.

We propose a heuristic which we call Priority-BFS, and show that it outperforms BFS as well as Lu-Ravi and Solis-Oba on grid graphs. We use this heuristic to generate initial solutions in the metaheuristic algorithms discussed in Section 6.

In Table 1 we compare the new heuristic against the standard breadth first search and the algorithms proposed by Lu-Ravi and Solis-Oba. The BFS algorithm is running the breadth first search from every vertex $v \in V$ and returning the best result. In this report, BFS algorithm will always denote this procedure. The data for Lu-Ravi and Solis-Oba shown in Table 1 are quoted from [1] (we did not implement those algorithms). Max-Priority-BFS is the Priority-BFS algorithm started from all vertices of G and then the best result is selected. This version of Priority-BFS runs in $O(n^2)$ time.

The pseudocode for algorithm Priority-BFS is given below. This algorithm maintains two sets T (the tree built so far) and Q (the set of leaves of the tree). Initially T is empty and Q contains a vertex with maximum degree. During the main while-loop the following invariant holds: T is the set of edges already in the final tree and Q is the set of leaves of T. At each iteration, node i in Q with the maximum number of neighbours outside T is selected and deleted from Q. All neighbours of node i outside of T are added to Q and T. At the end of the computation T is the final tree and Q is empty. It is very efficient to implement Q as a priority queue, where the key of a vertex is equal to $degree_G(v) - degree_T(v)$.

Algorithm 1 Priority-BFS

1: **function** PRIORITY-BFS(Graph G)   ▷ The MLST of G
2:     $start \leftarrow$ a vertex with maximum degree
3:     $T \leftarrow \emptyset$ ▷ T is the built tree
4:     $Q \leftarrow \emptyset$ ▷ empty priority queue with the leaves in T
5:     $push(Q, (start, degree(start)))$
6:     **while** $\neg empty(Q)$ **do**
7:         $i \leftarrow extract\_max(Q)$ ▷ The vertex with max $degree_G(v) - degree_T(v)$
8:         **for all** vertices v adjacent to i **do**
9:             $enqueue(Q, (v, degree_G(v) - degree_T(v)))$
10:            $T \leftarrow T \cup (i, v)$
11:        **end for**
12:    **end while**
13:    **return** T
14: **end function**

Table 1 shows that the performance of Priority-BFS is better than the other three algorithms for grid graphs of size $6 * 7$ and larger. We also observe that in many cases Priority-BFS finds the optimal solution.

6   Test Results

Tables 2 to 4 show the performance of all algorithms we implemented. All algorithms were run on exactly the same graphs and each table shows the performance on a different type of graph. For each graph, we ran 20 experiments. The Fujie and Fujie-PQ algorithms were tested only on small graphs.

Random graphs.   Table 2 shows the experiments for all implemented algorithms on random graphs with 30 to 50 nodes and density from 0.1 to 0.5. For dense as well as for sparse graphs the breadth first search achieves a relatively good solution. The priority-BFS (PBFS) algorithm outperformes the BFS algorithm on sparse random graphs. On dense random graphs (starting with density 0.2), the BFS algorithm achieves better solutions. Although it has been designed for grid graphs, in all our experiments the Max-PBFS algorithm outperformes the BFS as well as the PBFS algorithm. For random graphs the Max-PBFS algorithm gets very close to the optimum solution (on average, there is less than one leaf missing).

The Fujie algorithm is faster than the Fujie algorithm implemented using a priority queue (PQFujie) for dense graphs (usually with density > 0.2). For sparse graphs, the PQFujie algorithm is significantly faster than the Fujie algorithm.

d-regular graphs.   The BFS algorithm gives better results for d-regular graphs than the Priority-BFS algorithm. However, the MaxPBFS algorithm outperformes the BFS algorithm. We were only able to do limited experiments, because larger graphs take too long for the Fujie and PQFujie algorithms. On those experiments in Table 3, the

| Graph | | | | | Priority- | Max- | lower | |
n	m	BFS	Lu-Ravi	Solis-Oba	BFS	Priority-BFS	bound	optimum
3	3	*6	*6	*6	*6	*6	4	6
	4	7	*8	*8	*8	*8	6	8
	5	9	*10	*10	*10	*10	8	10
	6	11	*12	*12	*12	*12	10	12
	7	13	*14	*14	*14	*14	11	14
	8	15	*16	*16	*16	*16	13	16
	9	17	*18	*18	*18	*18	15	18
4	4	8	8	8	8	*9	8	9
	5	10	10	10	10	*11	11	11
	6	12	*14	*14	13	13	14	14
	7	14	15	*16	14	15	15	16
	8	16	*18	*18	17	*18	18	18
	9	18	19	*21	19	20	21	21
5	5	12	13	13	13	*14	14	14
	6	14	17	16	17	17	18	18
	7	16	19	18	19	*20	20	20
	8	18	21	20	21	*23	23	23
	9	20	25	23	25	26	27	27
6	6	16	21	19	18	21	22	22
	7	18	24	22	*26	*26	26	26
	8	20	27	25	*30	*30	30	30
	9	22	30	28	32	33	34	34
7	7	20	27	26	27	*29	27	29
	8	22	31	30	*33	*33	33	33
	9	24	35	34	37	37	39	39
8	8	24	35	34	*38	*38	38	38
	9	26	40	39	42	42	45	45
9	9	28	45	43	47	48	51	51

Table 1: *comparing Priority-BFS to Solis-Oba, Lu-Ravi and BFS on complete grid graphs. The * symbol indicates that the value is otimal.*

Fujie algorithm performs better than the PQFujie algorithm. This might be due to the fact that the distance between any two vertices is relatively near, in other words, the graph is too closely connected. Similar than the dense random graphs, here the selection process of the Fujie algorithm is very efficient.

Small complete grid graphs. On small grid graphs, a breadth-first search gives extremely poor results. The BFS algorithm finds only 35% of the number of leaves possible on a 9 by 9 grid. In general, a BFS algorithm gives poor results on any type of sparse or grid graph. However, the PBFS as well as the Max-PBFS algorithms find very good solutions, which are in some cases the optimum solution.

Small incomplete grid graphs. The experiments for small incomplete grid graphs have been made on n x m graphs with k removed edges, where $k = \frac{2nm}{10}, k = 2 * \frac{2nm}{10}, k = 3 * \frac{2nm}{10}$. We denote these three cases as case (1), (2) and (3) respectively. As Table 4 shows, the PBFS algorithm always gives as least as good results as the BFS algorithm. In case (1), the PBFS algorithm gives significantly better results than BFS. Note also, that MaxPBFS gives even better results than BFS for cases (1) and (2).

The PQFujie algorithm finds the optimum solution significantly faster than the Fujie algorithm in all three cases. For some experiments, we could not finish the Fujie algorithm, because it did not find the solution in a reasonable time.

Graph		BFS	PBFS	MaxPBFS	Opt.	Fujie		PQFujie	
n	p	sol.	sol.	sol.		prob.	time	prob.	time
30	0.1	17.10	17.55	18.60	18.95	19649.9	1.87	189.9	**0.01**
	0.2	21.20	21.60	22.95	23.55	15969.4	1.77	2856.6	**0.24**
	0.3	23.95	23.85	25.00	25.45	4364.5	0.62	3151.0	**0.28**
	0.4	25.10	24.50	26.00	26.35	1363.9	0.22	1678.9	**0.16**
	0.5	26.50	25.65	26.95	27.05	373.9	**0.07**	678.2	0.07
40	0.1	24.65	25.50	27.15	28.05	940001.3	142.45	3949.2	**0.48**
	0.2	30.50	30.20	32.15	33.40	31268.5	**5.73**	37893.5	10.74
	0.3	33.15	32.50	34.30	35.05	18828.6	4.22	19691.5	**4.04**
	0.4	35.05	34.50	35.75	36.20	5733.2	1.60	7029.3	**1.20**
	0.5	35.95	35.30	36.45	37.00	852.7	**0.28**	3297.9	0.58
50	0.1	33.00	34.50	36.90	38.10	14895916.4	2904.82	126355.3	**116.07**
	0.2	39.90	39.75	41.65	43.25	228427.2	**62.76**	343507.3	920.63
	0.3	42.90	42.10	44.05	44.95	85692.5	**30.85**	137992.6	154.82
	0.4	44.60	43.75	45.10	46.00	15393.0	6.76	17802.2	**5.14**
	0.5	45.90	45.00	46.35	47.00	1121.5	**0.61**	9049.7	2.68
60	0.4	54.40	53.50	55.20	56.05	28699.5	20.28	32174.6	**17.15**
	0.5	55.75	54.70	56.10	56.70	17326.9	**14.88**	30410.5	19.41
	0.6	56.40	55.45	56.95	57.00	3094.9	3.37	4804.0	**2.76**

Table 2: *experiments on small random graphs*

Graph		BFS	PBFS	MaxPBFS	Opt.	Fujie		PQFujie	
n	d	sol.	sol.	sol.		prob.	time	prob.	time
30	3	13.55	13.20	14.95	15.95	6935.7	0.82	6383.0	**0.77**
	4	17.25	17.15	18.75	20.00	11920.8	1.20	7351.0	**0.71**
	5	19.45	18.75	20.40	22.00	22756.2	**2.88**	21934.2	6.30
40	3	17.60	17.40	19.70	21.00	72643.4	**11.59**	50680.7	34.38
	4	22.20	22.60	24.90	26.40	242353.0	**37.67**	138030.6	129.00

Table 3: *experiments on small d-regular graphs*

Graph			BFS	PBFS	MaxPBFS	Opt.	Fujie		PQ-Fujie	
n	m	k	solution	solution	solution		subprob.	time	subprob.	time
4	4	3	7.75	7.90	**8.50**	**8.50**	273.5	0.01	36.4	0.00
		6	6.95	6.95	**7.10**	**7.10**	105.5	0.00	5.8	0.00
		9	5.80	**5.80**	**5.80**	**5.80**	18.0	0.00	1.0	0.00
	5	4	9.80	10.00	**10.50**	**10.50**	1038.6	0.05	58.3	0.00
		8	8.75	8.80	**9.10**	**9.10**	276.3	0.01	11.6	0.00
		12	7.40	**7.40**	**7.40**	**7.40**	22.0	0.00	1.0	0.00
	6	5	11.45	11.45	12.45	**12.55**	4917.4	0.35	126.9	0.01
		10	10.10	10.30	10.40	**10.55**	596.6	0.04	22.8	0.00
		15	**8.40**	**8.40**	**8.40**	**8.40**	26.0	0.00	1.0	0.00
	7	6	13.20	13.45	14.40	**14.55**	15063.6	1.24	308.1	0.02
		12	12.60	12.70	13.05	**13.10**	1198.5	0.09	31.2	0.00
		18	**9.40**	**9.40**	**9.40**	**9.40**	30.0	0.00	1.0	0.00
	8	6	15.05	15.60	16.75	**17.10**	137288.5	13.58	1048.5	0.07
		12	13.85	14.15	14.75	**14.85**	5864.0	0.57	110.3	0.01
		18	12.60	12.60	**12.65**	**12.65**	196.6	0.01	5.1	0.00
	9	7	17.45	17.80	19.15	**19.25**	369687.5	42.97	1253.0	0.10
		14	14.95	15.60	16.15	**16.25**	39439.0	4.39	240.4	0.02
		21	13.00	13.00	13.25	**13.35**	302.6	0.03	12.7	0.00
5	5	5	11.05	12.10	12.85	**13.00**	12814.7	0.97	288.7	0.01
		10	10.55	10.60	**11.25**	**11.25**	1263.7	0.09	42.3	0.00
		15	9.05	9.05	**9.10**	**9.10**	55.35	0.00	2.3	0.00
	6	6	13.20	14.65	15.75	**16.15**	58798.9	5.51	541.2	0.03
		12	12.85	13.00	13.70	**13.95**	6298.5	0.57	80.8	0.00
		18	10.85	**10.95**	**10.95**	**10.95**	152.9	0.01	4.5	0.00
	7	7	15.90	17.25	18.35	**18.65**	448718.5	49.02	2665.5	0.22
		14	15.20	16.00	16.75	**16.85**	15409.8	1.66	118.5	0.01
		21	12.40	12.65	**12.80**	**12.80**	206.0	0.02	16.9	0.00
	8	8	17.80	19.90	21.10	**21.60**	3046231.0	431.51	5686.0	0.81
		16	16.70	18.40	19.20	**19.40**	41295.5	5.74	302.8	0.03
		24	14.75	15.05	**15.45**	**15.45**	435.4	0.05	39.5	0.00
	9	9	19.90	21.85	23.50	**24.30**	n/A	n/A	22766.8	6.42
		18	18.35	20.25	21.05	**21.40**	203402.0	30.06	731.4	0.07
		27	17.60	18.00	**18.20**	**18.20**	2032.6	0.29	43.6	0.00
6	6	7	15.20	17.50	19.40	**19.80**	782113.7	104.64	2584.6	0.27
		14	14.90	16.30	17.30	**17.50**	30565.8	3.40	152.2	0.01
		21	13.90	14.20	**14.50**	**14.50**	612.9	0.07	31.2	0.00
	7	8	17.10	20.45	22.45	**23.15**	n/A	n/A	8830.9	1.26
		16	18.10	19.10	20.40	**20.70**	417144.8	55.57	392.5	0.04
		24	15.35	16.10	**16.65**	**16.65**	5465.7	0.74	67.9	0.01
	8	10	20.15	24.60	26.25	**26.70**	n/A	n/A	49101.9	38.08
		20	19.70	21.50	22.40	**22.80**	2114803.7	346.82	985.8	0.13
		30	16.85	17.25	**17.90**	**17.90**	4089.0	0.68	66.1	0.01

Table 4: *experiments on small incomplete grid graphs*

References

[1] Tetsuya Fujie, "An exact algorithm for the maximum leaf spanning tree problem", *Computers & Operations Research*, vol. 30, pp. 1932–1944, 2003.

[2] Lu H and Ravi R, "Approximating maximum leaf spanning trees in almost linear time", *Journal of Algorithms*, vol. 29, pp. 132-41, 1998.

[3] Solis-Oba, "2-approximation algorithm for finding a spanning tree with maximum number of leaves", *Lecture Notes in Computer Science*, vol. 1461, pp. 441-52, 1998.

[4] M. R. Garey, D. S. Johnson, "Computers and Intractability: A guide to the theory of NP-completeness", *W. H. Freeman, San Francisco*, 1979.

[5] G. Galbiati, F. Maffioli, A. Morzenti, "A short note on the approximability of the maximum leaves spanning tree problem", *Information Processing Letters 52*, pp. 45-49, 1994.

[6] E. W. Dijkstra, "Self-stabilizing systems in spite of distributed control", *Comm. ACM*, vol. 17, pp. 643-644, 1974.

A Programming Language with Role-Based Access Control

Asad Ali and Maribel Fernández

Department of Computer Science, King's College London
Strand, London WC2R 2LS, United Kingdom
{asad.2.ali,maribel.fernandez}@kcl.ac.uk

Abstract. We describe the design and implementation of a programming language with primitives for the specification of access control policies. Access control policies specify the way users can access resources. Our language provides primitives to facilitate the specification of policies using the Role-Based Access Control model, one of the most popular access control models in use currently. The language aims to simplify the writing of access control policies in software systems.

1 Introduction

This paper is concerned with implementing access control at programming language level. The objectives of an access control system are often described in terms of protecting system resources against inappropriate or undesired user access. Control of access in a computer system is a very important issue in computer science.

Most organisations, from multinational companies to a family home, are organised in such a way as to differentiate and categorise the members within them. So, any computer system designed for these organisations will need to implement features which distinguish the access rights that each user member has on the services or resources within the system. When there is a request for a service or resource, two main issues arise. The system must check which user triggered the request (for instance, a user may be a person, a company, or a program), and whether they have permission to gain access to this service or resource. Thus, an implementation of access control requires a formal specification of the rights associated to users in relation to resources. For this, several formalisms have been proposed to express access control policies, such as first order logic (see, for instance, [2]) or rewriting systems (see, for instance, [4]). Also, several models of access control have been defined, from simple access control lists (or matrices) giving for each user the list of authorised operations on resources, to more abstract models, such as the Role-Based Access Control (RBAC) model [6] which associates one or more roles to each user and associates to each role a list of privileges (or rights) to access resources.

Usually, programmers implement access control policies into systems based on security specifications provided by a security administrator. The security administrator is not required to have a good understanding of programming, therefore checking that

13

the security requirements have been met can be a complex process. Also, the programming effort for implementing access control policies is high, as often the language the software system is written in does not have any features to simplify this task.

Programming languages are a powerful way to express complex structures and relationships. Therefore, a language-based approach to implementing access control is natural in order to express a wide range of policies. In this paper, we describe the design and implementation of a programming language with primitives to specify access control. In this way, the access control policy can be written in the same language as the software application which defines the resources and operations associated to them, and security restrictions can be automatically enforced by the run-time system, thus reducing the programming effort. However, although the policy is written using the same language, it is separate from the rest of the program, facilitating in this way modular design of software applications with access control.

We define a block structured programming language called Access Control Language, or acl for short, where resources are objects, and the operations of interest are methods defined for these objects. The access restrictions become restrictions on the invocation of methods, which will be enforced by the programming language implementation.

To specify the restrictions on the access to resources, in acl we use the RBAC model. An access control policy therefore consists of a set of users, each associated to one or more roles, and a set of privileges for each role. The policy is specified using special purpose classes in the language; we give examples in the next sections.

Once the access control policy is specified in acl, the implementation of the language ensures that the access to resources respects the constraints imposed by policy, in a way that is transparent to the programmer. In other words, programmers do not have to write code to restrict access to resources, this is done directly by the implementation of the language.

A first implementation of the language defined in this paper has been developed by the first author.

There have been some previous proposals for language-based access control using RBAC, for instance the language proposed by Jajodia [10], which is less expressive than our language, the language described in [8], which is not as abstract as our proposal, and the proposal to weave access control policies into a programming language using aspect-oriented techniques, described in [16].

Overview of the paper. In the next section we give the preliminary notions that are needed in the rest of the paper. Section 3 defines our programming language with access control, and Section 4 briefly describes the implementation of the language. We conclude the paper in Section 5.

2 Background

2.1 Access Control

Access Control is the task of making sure a user or process accesses only resources which they are authorised to access [5]. We can see that this will require two things: to

14

be able to distinguish the user or process requesting access, and to check if they have the right to access the resource (i.e., to perform a specific operation or obtain a specific service). We briefly define below some key terms and concepts which are commonly used when discussing access control.

- **Subject** or **user**: An active entity, generally in the form of a person, process, or device that requests access to resources (see below) or changes the system state [11].
- **Object** or **resource**: An entity that contains or receives information. Access to an object usually means access to the information which that object contains. Typical objects are records, fields (in a database record), blocks, pages, files, directories, directory trees, process, and programs, as well as processors, video displays, keyboards, clocks, printers, and network nodes. Devices such as switches, disc drives, relays, and mechanical components connected to a computer system may also be included in the category of objects [11].
- **Operation** or **action**: An active process invoked by a subject; for example, when an online banking user successfully logs in, the control program operating on the user's behalf is a process, but the subject can initiate more than one operation such as a balance enquire or a bank transfer [6].
- **Permission** or **privilege**: The authorisation to perform some action in the system on objects. The term usually refers to some combination of object and operation, where that particular operation is allowed on that particular object. A particular operation used on two different objects represents two distinct permissions, and by the same notion, two different operations applied to a single object represent two distinct permissions. For example, a bank teller may have permissions to execute debit and credit operations on customer records through transactions, while an accountant may execute debit and credit operations on the general ledger, which consolidates the bank's accounting data [6].
- **Access Control Policy**: The high level rules specifying how access is managed [13]. It describes the user and the circumstances in which access may be granted to the information or resource.
- **Access Control Mechanism**: Done at hardware or software level, this is where the access control limitations described in the policies are implemented [13].

2.2   Access Control Models

An Access Control Model includes a description of the main entities in the system (usually, subjects, resources, privileges) and the way access to resources is controlled. Rougly speaking, an access control security policy describes a specific system, with a set of users and their access privileges. Formal specifications of access control policies allow proof of properties on the security provided by the access control system being designed [13]. Thus, they are useful for proving theoretical limitations of a system. Access control models bridge the gap in abstraction between access control policy and access control mechanism [9]. Access control mechanisms are designed to remain faithful to the properties of the chosen model.

There are several models for access control. Below we discuss three which have influenced our design:

15

- **Discretionary access control**: where the owner of each resource (files/data) decides what the access rights to the resource are. In this model, there is the concept of every resource having an owner, and the owner specifies the permissions (such as read or write) to the resource. Often, discretionary access control models are implemented using access control lists, or an access control matrix.
- **Mandatory access control**: where access policies are determined by the system with multiple levels of access. In this model, access control is regulated and enforced by a central authority, and not by owners of objects and so they cannot change the access rights. This model is usually multi-level, where access rights are divided into levels and subjects and objects are given a level, and subjects can only access objects on the relevant level. Subjects are active entities or processes that request access to objects, and objects are usually information stores [13].
- **Role-based access control**: where access is determined by the user's role within the system. In the RBAC model, users are given roles based on their position and responsibilities in the organisation. Access control limitations are based on the user's role. User membership into roles can be taken away easily and changing a member's role can be established as job assignments dictate. Role associations can be established when new operations are put in place, and old operations can be removed as organisational functions change over time [13]. This makes it much simpler and easier to manage access control because roles can be updated without updating each user's access individually.

Other models have been proposed in the literature, including dynamic models that are well suited to distributed, rapidly changing environments, such as the model described in [3]. We will not consider these in this paper - dynamic models will be the subject of future work. In the next subsection we compare the three models described above.

2.3   Comparison of Access Control Models

Discretionary Access Control (DAC) has some weaknesses, for instance, systems based on DAC may allow users to copy information from one object into another, so there is no control on the information flow in a system. Also, since privileges are associated individually to each user, DAC policies are harder to write and maintain. Mandatory Access Control (MAC) tries to solve the issues in DAC, specifically the problem of controlling information flow, by using security levels. Still, MAC policies suffer from some of the problems of DAC, in particular with respect to maintenance.

Role Based Access Control (RBAC) has several advantages. Firstly, in RBAC it is easier to manage access control because roles can be updated without updating each user's access individually. This is due to the way the task of user authorisation is broken down [13]. Firstly, users are assigned roles, and then authorisations to access objects are assigned to roles. Some examples of the simplification include: when a new user joins the organisation, the administrator only needs to grant them the roles corresponding to their job; when a user's job changes, the administrator simply has to change the roles associated with that user. Secondly, it allows for *Hierarchical Roles*; roles can be specified in a hierarchy, so that access rights can be classified by level and child nodes in the hierarchy can inherit permissions from the parent node. This further simplifies authorisation management. Thirdly, it has the concept of *Least Privilege*; roles allow a user to sign on with the least privilege required for the particular task (s)he needs to perform. Users assigned powerful roles do not need to exercise them until those privileges are actually needed. This minimizes the danger of damage due to inadvertent errors or Trojan Horses [13]. Lastly, it has *Separation of Duties*; the notion that no user should be given enough privileges to be able to misuse the system on their own. For example, someone who authorises a pay check should not be the same person who can prepare them. This can be imposed statically by defining roles which cannot be executed by the same user, or dynamically by imposing the control at access time. To help understand the dynamic way of imposing separation of duty, consider an example of the two-person rule where the first user must be an authorised user and the second must be any user different from the first.

However, there are limitations to the current descriptions of the RBAC model. There is still some work to be done to cover all the different requirements that real world scenarios may present [13]. For instance, the simple hierarchical relationship as intended in current proposals may not be sufficient to model the different kinds of relationships that can occur. Also, there is a lack of mechanisms to adapt policy to changes in the system, such as when a user leaves or there is a new role in the organisation. Despite these limitations, RBAC is very widely used, especially in commercial systems. Role-based policies represent a promising direction and a useful paradigm for many commercial and government organisations. For these reasons we have chosen to design and implement a programming language with primitives for the specification of access control policies in the RBAC model.

3   Programming Language Design

In this section we describe the design of a programming language with access control primitives, which we call Access Control Language, or simply acl. The implementation of the language is described in the next section.

3.1   Design Issues

In order to design and create a programming language, we must specify three things:

1. Syntax: described as a grammar, this defines the form of programs; how the symbols are built, put together and combined to form a syntactically correct program.
2. Semantics: giving the meaning of programs i.e. what they do when they are executed.
3. Implementation: the software system which reads in the program and executes it in the machine, and an extra set of tools such as editing and debugging tools.

In the design of the language, there are many issues to consider in the areas of readability, writeability and reliability [17]. The issues directly related to the RBAC language are control statements, data types/structures and syntax considerations (such as identifier forms and keywords), affecting readability; abstraction, related to write-ability; and type checking and exception handling, related to reliability.

The main aims of the language are to minimise the amount of programming knowledge and the amount of effort required in order to write code to perform access control. These can be achieved in many ways. Firstly, having a high level of abstraction can help to achieve both aims. Abstraction is defined as being able to define and use complicated structures in a way that ignores many of the low level details [17]. A common example of abstraction is in high level languages, where one line of code in a high level language translates to many lines of machine code. So, if the language is highly abstract, it will be more readable and it will be easier and quicker to write code. Building on this, the syntax can be made abstract in such a way as it resembling natural language. This will immensely help in readability and reduce the effort needed to learn the language.

3.2 The programming language acl

The language and the application as a whole provide the basic functions required to enable access control, more precisely, to restrict users from performing some methods on a class. The acl language supports role-based access control, thus, programs will specify users, roles and classes, and the assignment of roles to users and classes to roles. Therefore, the methods in a class (which are the resources to be protected) will only be allowed to be run by certain roles, and so the user must have the required role to be able to run the method.

The language acl has a small number of basic types and constructs in order to simplify writing code in it. There is just one Access Control class generated to implement access control into a software system, in an effort to simplify the implementation and minimise the impact of implementing access control into that system.

In the rest of this section we describe three main aspects of the language:

– The syntax and semantics of the programming language constructs, in particular the constructs that allow programmers to specify access control policies (as described above).
– The Access Control class which handles the access control for the software system which requires access control; this is automatically generated by the language implementation, freeing programmers from the task of writing code to enforce the access control policy.
– The technique used to implement the language, which is based on source code transformations and code generation (to ensure that the use of resources is compatible with the access control policy specification). A concrete implementation is discussed in the next section.

The language acl is implemented in Java, for Java: the whole application is written in Java and deals with Java source code.

Syntax and semantics The language definition is based on Java [7]. However, the current version of acl is not object oriented, yet it is block structured. Full object-orientation as seen in Java will be added in future work. In the current version of the language, the

18

reduced abstraction that results from the lack of object orientation is made up for by the use of simple, clear keywords in the language. The language includes the following primitive data types: integer, real, Boolean and strings. Then there are types for roles, users and classes.

All programs written in acl start with { and end with }.

In acl, users and roles are declared simply by writing *user* or *role* followed by the name. An example of how Users and Roles are declared is as follows:

user bob;
role nurse;

Roles are assigned by writing the name of the user followed by the use of the keyword *is*, and lastly the role to be assigned. An example of this is:

bob is nurse;

Finally, methods in classes are assigned to a role by writing the role name, followed by the keyword *access*, then the list of classes and methods to be assigned separated by a blank space. If only a class name is given, it is assumed that all its methods are included. For example:

nurse access class1 class2 class3;

Using just these three concepts, the syntax allows for access to be controlled.

We omit the syntax of the programming constructs (assignment, sequence, conditional, loops) which follow the conventions used in Java.

Generation of an Access Control Class For each program written in acl, an Access Control class will be generated to handle the control of access. The generation of this class is heavily linked to the implementation of the acl program. Firstly, there are tables to hold the users, the roles allocated to each user and the classes allocated to each role. All these tables will be filled in with details gathered from the acl program. Secondly, code will be generated to deal with user identification (login) when the software system is started. Thirdly, a lookup method will be implemented which will check if the user has the required rights to run a method.

Transformation and Generation of source code In the software system that requires access control, the source code will be modified so that every method that requires a controlled access calls the lookup method in the Access Control class first. This is to check if the user has the required rights to run the method. For this, the acl source code is parsed, and code is generated to check that only users with correct rights can access the methods that require access control.

Since acl is based on Java, to facilitate the parsing and tranformation of Java source code, an external library called BeautyJ (by Jens Gulden) has been used. It is a Java source code transformation tool which generates a clean, normalized representation of the code. The specific features which are of interest are the ability to identify methods in Java source code and to modify the code of these methods.

4 Implementation

There are two main ways in which to implement a programming language. One is compiling, and the other is interpreting. Compiling is transforming the source code from one form into another, usually a computer machine readable form [1]. The task of compiling is broken up into three parts: lexical analysis, parsing and code generation. During lexical analysis, the input program is read, grouping parts of it together to form tokens. Parsing is then checking the sequence of tokes for errors and converting the input program into another form, usually in the shape of a tree. Type checking can then take place at this stage. Then, code is generated (machine code, or code in another language).

The other implementation technique is interpreting, which is actually performing and executing the actions written in the language on some machine. An interpreter may be a program that either: executes the source code directly, translates source code into some efficient intermediate representation (code) and immediately executes this or explicitly executes stored precompiled code made by a compiler which is part of the interpreter system.

The implementation technique chosen for our language consists of a (pre)compilation into Java code. For this, a preprocessor has been written, consisting of a lexical analyser, symbol table generator, parser and a code modifier; see the class diagram in Figure 1. The first three of these work as in other similar compilers, however the main distinguishing features are that the preprocessor identifies users, roles, role assignments, and class to role assignments. The parser also creates and maintains the tables mentioned in Section 3.2. These are discussed in more detail below.

4.1 Implementing Tables

In the Access Control class which has to be generated, three tables are required.

User Table All the users are stored in a Java HashMap, which maps unique keys to values. The way in which this is achieved is by storing the name of the user as the unique key, and this maps to the word "user" which is stored as a string. This way we can be sure only unique users are stored. The users will be put into this HashMap every time a user is declared in the acl program; i.e., when the parser recognises a user declaration.

Role Assignment Table The roles assigned to each user are stored in another HashMap. The unique key is again the name of the user, and the value it is mapped to is the name of the role that is assigned to that user. The role assignments are put into this HashMap every time there is a role assignment in the acl program; i.e., when the parser recognises a role assignment.

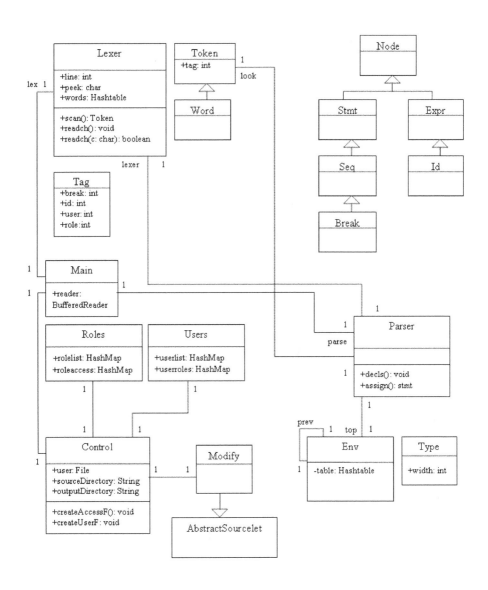

Fig. 1. Class diagram

21

Class Assignment Table The classes assigned to each role are stored in a third HashMap, except this time the unique key is the name of the role and the value to which this is mapped is a Java ArrayList, which will hold the name of all the classes that this role has access to. This way, a role can only be assigned classes one time. Currently, a role can access and run any of the methods in these specified classes (the selection of specific methods has not been implemented yet). The class to role assignments are put into this HashMap every time there is a classes to role assignment in the acl program; i.e., when the parser recognises a class assignment.

4.2   Code Modification

The source code of the software system that requires access control has to be modified. Code needs to be inserted to get the current user's name and to call the lookup method (discussed below) inside every method that has been flagged to be subject to access control. The programmer writing the main software system will flag every method that will be subject to access control, as some methods will always be needed for basic running of the system. In this way, only the flagged methods will have code inserted. The flag is the string '//access' (without the apostrophes). Code modification is achieved by using the BeautyJ library previously discussed. It uses special classes called sourcelets, which specify how to transform and optionally modify source code. The standard sourcelet provided in the library was extended to do two things:

- Firstly, it finds the main method and inserts the code to get the user's name, before doing anything else. It stores the user in a member field of the Access Control class.
- Secondly, it finds the methods that have the special flag in them and inserts the call to the lookup method. It does this by having an if statement, with the boolean return value of the lookup method as the condition, and the true branch being the code of the method, and the false branch throwing an IllegalArgumentException. This stops the method from running but does not terminate the main application.

4.3   Lookup Method

There is a lookup method which is called whenever a method is run, checking if the user can run that method. The lookup method is given the calling class as a parameter, meaning the class in which this method has been called. It works by first getting the role of the current user by checking the HashMap that contains the role assignments. Then, it gets the ArrayList of classes from the class to role assignment HashMap, and checks if this ArrayList contains the calling class parameter. If it contains the class parameter, it returns true otherwise it returns false.

Pseudocode for Lookup Method:

```
lookup(classname)
    user's role = role assignment table.get(current user);
    classes = class assignment table.get(user's role);
    if(classes contains classname)) return true;
    else return false;
```

5 Conclusions

In this paper, we have briefly described the design and implementation of a block structured programming language with primitives for the specification of access control policies following the Role-Based Access Control model. The basic features of the model have been implemented, specifically the concepts of roles, users and restricting access to methods, and these can be applied to any software system where there are multiple users.

In future work, we will extend the language to cover all the features of the Role-Based Access Control model; in particular, we will consider hierarchies of roles and verification of constraints such as separation of duties. We will also extend the block-structured kernel of the language in order to include all of the Java language. Further to this, we will investigate the use of richer access control models in our language, for instance the dynamic, event-based models proposed in [3].

References

1. A. V. Aho, M. S. Lam, R. Seth, J. D. Ullman, *Compilers Principles, Techniques and Tools*, Addison-Wesley, 2007.
2. S. Barker and P. Stuckey. Flexible access control policy specification with constraint logic programming. *ACM Trans. on Information and System Security*, 6(4):501–546, 2003.
3. C. Bertolissi, M. Fernández, and S. Barker. Dynamic event-based access control as term rewriting. In *Proc. of DBSEC'07)*, volume 4602 of *LNCS*. Springer-Verlag, 2007.
4. C. Bertolissi and M. Fernández. A Rewriting Framework for the Composition of Access Control Policies. In *Proc. of PPDP 2008*, ACM Press.
5. S. De Capitani di Vimercati, P. Samarati, S. Jajodia. *Policies, models, and languages for access control*, Volume 3433 of Lecture Notes in Computer Science, Springer, 2005.
6. D. Ferraiolo, D. Kuhn, R. Chandramouli. *Role-Based Access Control*, Computer Security Series, Artech House, 2003.
7. J. Gosling, B. Joy, and G. Steele. *The Java Language Specification*. Addison-Wesley, Reading, MA, 1996.
8. M. Hitchens, V. Varadharajan. *Tower: A language for Role Based Access Control*, Policies for Distributed Systems and Networks, Springer Berlin / Heidelberg, 2001.
9. V. C. Hu, D. F. Ferrialo, D. Rick Kuhn. *Assessment of Access Control Systems*, National Institute of Standards and Technology, 2006.
10. S. Jajodia, P. Samarati, V. Subrahmanian, *A logical Language for expressing authorizations*, Proceedings of the IEEE Symposium on Security and Information Privacy, Oakland CA, 1997.
11. National Computer Security Center (NCSC), *Glossary of Computer Security Terms*, Report NSCD-TG-004, Fort Meade, Md.: NCSC, 1988.
12. R. Kissel *Glossary of Key Information Security Terms*, NIST IR 7298, National Institute of Standards and Technology, 2006.
13. P. Samarati S. De Capitani di Vimercati, *Glossary of Computer Security Terms*, Foundations of Security Analysis and Design, Springer-Verlag, 2001.
14. R. C. Summers. *Secure Computing Threats and Safeguard*, McGraw-Hill, 1997.
15. R. S. Sandhu. *Transaction control expressions for separation of duties*, Fourth Annual Computer Security Application Conference, Orlando, FL, 1988.

16. A. Santana de Oliveira, E. Ke Wang, C. Kirchner and H. Kirchner. Weaving rewrite-based access control policies, *Proceedings of the 2007 ACM workshop on Formal methods in security engineering*, FMSE 2007, ACM Press, 2007.
17. R. W. Sebesta. *Concepts of Programming Languages*, Addison-Wesley, 2006.

Using Effect Systems for Automating Model Extraction

R. L. Crole (`R.Crole@mcs.le.ac.uk`) & A. Furniss (`mjf29@le.ac.uk`)

Department of Computer Science,
University of Leicester,
University Road,
Leicester,
LE1 7RH, U.K.

Abstract. We present a programming language called Do which has an effect system. Do is motivated by Wadler's extension of the computational lambda calculus. Do is specified by augmenting (the language of) the extension with a set of predefined effects and with provision for programmers to create their own application-specific effects. Do is accompanied by Dome (Do model extractor), a tool to extract models of Do programs for model-checking. Models are created with regard to a particular computational effect or set of effects. A *key difference* between our approach and previous approaches is that vertices in program graphs represent the *effect behaviour* of statements, rather than the statement itself.

1 Introduction

Model checking [10] is a verification technique that determines if a specification in a temporal logic such as linear temporal logic or computation tree logic holds for a model of a system, represented as a transition system consisting of states connected by transitions. Model checkers exhaustively search the possible states of the model in order to find a counter-example - a state path that demonstrates that the specification does not hold for the model.

As current model checkers can only represent a limited number of states and the number of states in a typical program is potentially very high, the construction of a considerably simplified abstract model is often required. When creating a model one must ensure that it is a correct representation of the program, in that the model displays every behaviour of interest contained within the program and does not introduce additional behaviour that is not present in the program. Models are often created by hand or with a user-defined translation table to directly translate a program into the model checker definition language, but these methods introduce the potential for human error. Techniques for automatically deriving models from programs are therefore desirable, and we pursue this goal here.

Our aim here is to present a method for creating models of the interactions of a computer program (and constituent threads) with the computer system state.

25

We are currently implementing this method in our Dome (Do Model Extractor) tool to allow the automatic generation of models of Do programs for the Spin model checker.

We proceed as follows: We review the relevant background literature in the next section. In Section 3 we explain some foundational properties of states, effects and dependencies. In Section 4 we specify an operational semantics for the Do language. In Section 5 we specify a graph extraction algorithm. In Section 7 we explain the model extraction process. Finally in Section 8 we draw our conclusions.

2 Background

2.1 Effect systems

Effect systems make explicit the effect of executing a statement or expression by incorporating details of the effects carried out by the statement into its type. As a consequence one is able to determine not only what the return or result type of a statement is, but also the actions that the statement will have upon the state of the system. Effects are annotated with a region to indicate which resource or part of a resource they act upon. The terminology stems from research into region-based memory management in which the heap is partitioned into sections called regions, and memory effects are annotated with the region they act upon. The term tag is also used (for example in [12]) to indicate the same type of annotation.

Lucassen and Gifford [11] describe an effect system with types, effects and regions, and effects of reading, writing or allocating memory locations. They give an operational semantics for their type and effect inference rules and introduce the idea of effect masking, in which effects that are local to an expression appear only in contexts in which they are observable. This is accomplished through a 'PRIVATE' expression that creates an anonymous region which is inaccessible after the expression or statement has finished executing.

Marino and Millstein [12] provide a framework for a generic effect system, and demonstrate how memory effects and transactional memory can be implemented in terms of their generic framework. They use sets of privileges defining which effects a given section of a program may carry out, and show how the privileges may be enforced during type-checking. Although the effect system here (and other effect systems in the literature) are oriented more towards the description of effects carried out by code rather than restriction using the notion of privileges, we can consider the set of privileges required by a given section of code equivalent to the set of effects that the code performs.

2.2 Computational Monads and Monadic Effect Systems

Moggi [13] introduces the notion of computation types. Given a type τ one also has a type $T\tau$ which designates computations which may deliver a result of

26

type τ. For example the type might be int and Tint $=$ int$_{\perp}$, the type of all programs that may be non-terminating but otherwise return an integer. In [13], Moggi considers non-deterministic computation, side-effects and continuations. Computation types allow many different types of computations and effects to be treated in a uniform manner, and forms the basis for the effect system described in [15]. Crole has investigated the use of computation types in giving semantics to IO effects [5], and there are connections between the IO semantics and the Do semantics seen in the current paper.

Wadler and Thiemann [15] modify an existing effect system to produce one based upon computation types by labelling each (standard) computation type with a set of effects so that a computation of type τ but with an *explicit* effect σ actually has type $T^\sigma\tau$. The semantics of the Do language is based upon the systems specified in this paper. Like [11], Wadler and Thiemann give a type and effect inference algorithm, in which type and effect reconstruction is performed by creating and solving systems of constraints.

2.3 Program slicing

A program slice consists of a subprogram that computes or performs computation using a specific variable or set of variables at a particular point in the program. This variable or set of variables and program location is referred to as the slicing criterion. Slices are either forward slices, which include all elements of the program that could be affected by the slicing criterion, or backward slices that include all elements of the program that could affect the computation of the slicing criterion. Techniques in the literature generally either perform static slicing to compute a slice for all possible execution traces of the program, or dynamic slicing to create a slice of all parts of the program that affect a specific execution trace. *The slicing criterion in this paper differs from those discussed elsewhere as it consists of a set of effects to include in the generated model.* To extract a model the original program is reduced to one that solely includes all possible paths that include effects contained within the slicing criterion – essentially a series of static backwards slices.

The most common approaches to static backwards slicing in the literature have been graph-based. Hatcliff et al [8] consider program slicing in the context of model production for their Bandera tool using a control-flow graph. They show how to extract slicing criteria from a LTL formula, and prove that their slicing algorithm preserves the properties of the model that satisfy the criteria, allowing an optimised model to be constructed for each formula.

Horwitz, Reps and Binkley [9] discuss program slicing using dependence graphs. They start with a description of slicing programs with a single procedure or function using a program dependence graph. Such graphs have an entry vertex, variable declaration and variable final use vertices for each variable in the procedure, along with data and control dependence edges. They then extend the program representation to a system dependence graph to allow slicing of programs with multiple procedures or functions by introducing function call site, formal in, formal out, actual in and actual out vertices, along with function call edges, parameter in and out edges. Their slicing algorithm operates in two stages. In the first stage the slice is computed by starting from the vertex representing the initial node of the slice, marking nodes that are either in the same function or are in functions that have called the function containing the initial node. In the second stage, the slicing algorithm traverses functions that are called by the function containing the starting point of the slice. The final slice is the union of the sets of vertices marked during the two stages.

Zhao [16] describes multi-threaded dependence graphs, an extension of the program dependence graphs used in methods of slicing sequential programs (most notably from [9]). Multi-threaded dependence graphs provide a thread dependence graph for each individual thread with edges to represent communication dependencies or synchronisation dependencies between threads. Communication dependencies occur when the result of a statement or expression in one thread is influenced by the result of a statement or expression in another thread. Synchronisation dependencies occur when the concurrency features of Java such as notify(), wait() and join() are used to synchronise threads.

2.4   A Note on Implementation Details

Appel and Palsberg [1] provide an overview of compiler design and related issues including type checking and symbol tables, which are an important aspect of both the model extractor and interpreter. They distinguish between imperative and functional symbol tables. Imperative symbol tables perform destructive updates on a single instance of the symbol table and have an 'undo' stack that restores the previous state upon leaving the scope. Functional symbol tables create a new instance of the symbol table when adding an entry, allowing the previous version to be restored upon leaving the scope. Strategies for efficiently implementing the different types of symbol table are also discussed. Muchnick [14] provides a further in-depth discussion of symbol tables, including their implementation using hash-tables for languages with different scoping rules.

The lexer and parser have been generated using Flex and Bison. During this process, the Flex documentation [7], Bison documentation [3] and C++ Flex/Bison example by Timo Bingmann [2] were useful.

3   States, Effects and Dependencies

Our aim is to present a method for creating models of the interactions of a computer program (and constituent threads) with the computer system state. We consider a system with concurrently and autonomously executing program threads, which carry out *computations* that may or may not interact with the state of the system. Here regions are labels that are used to identify system state such as memory locations or other system resources. An effect describes how a computation changes the state of the system or depends upon the state of the system. Each effect acts upon one or more regions. We further distinguish between *atomic* effects, which are 'indivisible' primitive effects on the system, and *composite* effects which are composed of two or more primitive effects.

Effects describe transformations in the state of the system. We write $\sigma(s)$ to denote the result of updating the state of the system s with effect σ, and $\sigma_1 ; \sigma_2$ to denote composition of effects. For all effects σ_1 and σ_2, $\sigma_1 ; \sigma_2(s) = \sigma_2(\sigma_1(s))$. We define traces of effects in a conventional manner. A *trace* is a sequence of effects $\sigma_1 \rightarrow \sigma_2 \rightarrow \ldots \rightarrow \sigma_{n-1} \rightarrow \sigma_n$ where n is 0 in the case of the *empty trace*. The *concatenation* of traces is defined as expected.

One of the key aspects of our approach concerns the dependence or independence of effects. An effect σ_1 is dependent upon another effect σ_2 if the result of carrying out σ_1 can alter depending upon how or if σ_2 has previously been carried out. For example, consider a system with memory locations, a *get* effect that describes accessing a memory location and a *set* effect that describes updating a location. The result of accessing a memory location is dependent upon the value that has previously been stored there, so the *get* effect is dependent upon the *set* effect. However, the converse does not hold, as the result of updating a memory location will be the same irrespective of how the location has previously been been accessed. We write the relationship of dependency as $\sigma_1 \dashv_{dep} \sigma_2$.

Once we understand the relationships between effects, we can use them to reason about the result on system state of performing computation; in particular we include effects and effect dependencies as "first class" citizens in the Do Language. To do this we first need to introduce effect and dependency sets. The effect set of a trace is the set of effects that the trace performs (in a similar manner to the concept of a sort in CCS). Note that we can consider a computation to be a trace of length 1, in which case the effect set is simply the effect of the computation. The *effect set* of a trace $t = \sigma_1 \rightarrow \ldots \rightarrow \sigma_n$ is $\mathit{Eff}(t) = \{\sigma_i \mid \sigma_i \in t\}$. Given the effect set we can now define the dependency set, which is essentially the set of effects which may influence the outcome of the trace. The dependency set is constructed from the set of all effects upon which any effect in the effect set of the trace is dependent upon. The *dependency set* of a trace t is $\mathit{Dep}(t) = \{\sigma' \mid \sigma \in \mathit{Eff}(t), \sigma \dashv^+_{dep} \sigma'\}$ where $^+$ denotes transitive closure.

To return to the previous example of memory locations, if we wanted to create a model of memory accesses it would not be enough to simply include all of the get effects in the model, as we cannot accurately represent the result of memory access without also including the effects that set the contents of the location. When we decide to include a type of effect in the model, we must also include all of the effects that it is dependent upon. Due to the nondeterministic nature of concurrent execution we cannot know what order the effects of the various threads will be performed, and it is difficult or impossible to know which sections of program code can be executed concurrently with each other. In the interest of simplicity, we do not attempt to determine which sections of the program may be run concurrently, and instead consider potential interactions between all instances across the entire program of the effects in question.

We include the notion of effect environments in the semantics of Do ranged over by β, a function from the set of identifiers to the set of effects. β_{id} denotes the effect environment β with the identifier id removed from its domain.

The notion of effect dependencies is important because it enables the system to determine which effects need to be included in extracted models when slicing. We determine the dependencies of an effect using an effect graph, with vertices representing effects and edges representing dependencies. We define the dependency set of a statement or expression to be the union of the dependency sets of each effect contained within the type of the expression or statement. The dependency set is determined using a breadth-first search to calculate the transitive closure of effect dependencies, following dependency edges and marking nodes to avoid infinite loops. Once the set cannot be expanded further, the effects represented by the marked nodes form the dependency set.

4 The Do Language

We have so far discussed effects as a mathematical abstraction, but we now present concrete effects in the context of the Do programming language. Do is a simple functional programming language with a conventional syntax and semantics, but with the addition of an *effect system*. Types τ range over integers, booleans, a unit type, and functions. Given a countable set Id of identifiers, the (raw/untyped) Do expressions and statements are specified by

$$V ::= \underline{b} \mid \underline{i} \mid () \mid id \; values$$

$$values ::= \epsilon \mid V \; values$$

$$E ::= \underline{b} \mid \underline{i} \mid id \mid uop \; E \mid E \; bop \; E \mid E \; E$$

$$uop ::= \sim \mid \neg \; \text{and} \; bop ::= \; + \mid - \mid / \mid * \mid \&\& \mid \|\|$$

$$S ::= \texttt{skip} \mid \texttt{new} \; \tau \; id \mid \texttt{get} \; id \mid \texttt{set} \; id \; := E \mid \texttt{let} \; id \; := \; E \; \texttt{in} \; S \mid S \; ; \; S$$

$$\mid \texttt{if} \; E \; \texttt{then} \; S \mid \texttt{if} \; E \; \texttt{then} \; S_1 \; \texttt{else} \; S_2 \mid \texttt{fun} \; id \; params \; = S \mid \texttt{return} \; E$$

$$params ::= \epsilon \mid id : \tau \; params$$

Do has a 'small-step' operational semantics. This is an adaptation and extension of the Effect language presented in [15] (and also motivated by the Monad language loc. cit.). Do is call-by-value to simplify the order and sequence of evaluation (and hence simplify the extracted models of programs).[1] Other common constructs such as conditional statements are also introduced, along with the ability to declare new user effects and dependencies between them. To specify

---

[1] A simple form of concurrency has been introduced into the language with the addition of a `split` effect, which will cause a function to be used as the entry point for a new thread running concurrently with the existing one—the details are omitted from this paper.

the semantics we define a (countable) set of *locations* *Loc* to be a subset of the (countable) set of *Id* of identifiers. A *store* is a function from locations to the set *Val* of values. A semantic effect [15] f takes the form $new_{\mathit{eff}}(l)$, $get_{\mathit{eff}}(l)$ or $set_{\mathit{eff}}(l)$ where l is a location.

The operational semantics is specified by using evaluation contexts $\mathcal{C}$ (see for example [6]).

$$\mathcal{C} ::= [\,] \mid uop\ \mathcal{C} \mid \mathcal{C}\ bop\ E \mid V\ bop\ \mathcal{C} \mid \mathcal{C}\ E \mid V\ \mathcal{C}$$
$$\mid \texttt{if } \mathcal{C} \texttt{ then } S \mid \texttt{if } \mathcal{C} \texttt{ then } S_1 \texttt{ else } S_2$$
$$\mid \texttt{set } id := \mathcal{C} \mid \texttt{let } id := \mathcal{C} \texttt{ in } S$$
$$\mid \mathcal{C}\ ;\ E \mid V\ ;\ \mathcal{C} \mid \texttt{return } \mathcal{C}$$

The operational semantics [4] transitions take the form $(s, \beta, \dashv_{dep})$, $X \xrightarrow{f} (s', \beta', \dashv_{dep}')$, X' where X is an expression or a statement, generalising the transitions of [15]. In the case that no changes occur to s, β, or $\dashv_{dep}$ then we write simply $X \longrightarrow X'$. Much of the semantics is standard, but some of the non-standard transitions are given in Figure 1.

$$\frac{}{(s, \beta, \dashv_{dep}),\ \texttt{new } \tau\ l \xrightarrow{new_{\mathit{eff}}(l)} (s \cup \{l \to 0\}, \beta, \dashv_{dep}),\ ()} \ new\ [l \notin dom(s)]$$

$$\frac{}{(s_l \cup \{l \to V\},\ \beta, \dashv_{dep}),\ \texttt{get } l \xrightarrow{get_{\mathit{eff}}(l)} (s_l \cup \{l \to e\}, \beta, \dashv_{dep}),\ V} \ get$$

$$\frac{}{(s_l \cup \{l \to V\}, \beta, \dashv_{dep}),\ \texttt{set } l := V' \xrightarrow{set_{\mathit{eff}}(l)} (s_l \cup \{l \to V'\}, \beta, \dashv_{dep}),\ ()} \ set$$

$$\frac{}{\texttt{let } id = V \texttt{ in } S \to S[x := V]} \ let_2$$

$$\frac{}{id\ V_1\ \ldots\ V_a \to S[params := \boldsymbol{V}]} \ funcall\ [\texttt{fun } id\ params := S]$$

$$\frac{}{\texttt{return } V \to V} \ return$$

The rule for evaluation contexts is

$$\frac{X \xrightarrow{f} X'}{(s, \beta, \dashv_{dep}),\ \mathcal{C}[e] \xrightarrow{f} (s, \beta, \dashv_{dep}),\ \mathcal{C}[e']} \ evcxt$$

Fig. 1. Operational Semantics for Do

---

5   A Graph Extraction Algorithm and Implementation

The remainder of this paper focuses on an example program P given in Figure 2.

```
new int a;
new int b;
new int c;

fun fib2 :  int x :  int y :  int i :  int = {
(1)       if i = 0 then (2) return y;
(3)       if i = 1 then (4) return x + y;
(5)       set a := x + y;
(7)       set b := (6) get a + y;
(8)       set c := i - 2;
(14)      return (12) (13) fib2 (9) (get a) (10) (get b) (11) (get c)
};

fun fib :  int n :  int = {
(15)      let z := n - 1 in
(16)      return (17) (18) fib2 0 1 z
};

fun main :  unit d :  unit = {
(19)      return (20) (21) fib 42
};
```

Fig. 2. Progam P

One of the key aims during model creation is to limit the number of states and transitions in order to ensure the tractability of queries upon the model. To achieve this we create a control-flow graph representation of effects carried out by the program and then select a slice (or subgraph) that includes only behaviour matching a specified set of effects.

Our graph representation is based upon the system dependence graphs introduced in [9], although it has some important differences. While vertices in the system dependence graphs created by Horwitz et al represent statements themselves, we create graphs in which vertices represent the *behaviour* of the statement or expression in the form of its effect. Such graphs are therefore fundamentally a representation of the interaction of the program with system state rather than statements of the the program itself.

We introduce an additional type of edge, corresponding to the sequential order in which the effects represented by the vertices are performed. Unlike the system dependence graphs outlined in [9] we do not consider data-flow. As a result, the creation and slicing of the control-flow graphs described here is somewhat simpler than system dependence graphs, as we do not create variable definition and last-use vertices, or formal and actual parameter in and out vertices.

However, the availability of data-flow information would enable a reduction in the number of transitions and states in the model. In the method outlined here we do not maintain a record of the state of regions, such as the contents of memory locations. When considering a statement such as set $a := b + 32$ we record only that an instance of the set effect has occurred; the value actually stored in the memory location represented by region a is not included in the model.

On one hand this reduces the amount of information stored for each state, and therefore the amount of memory required, and as a result improving the chance of creating a tractable model. However, as a consequence of this lack of state we cannot evaluate the condition of conditional statements during model-checking, so deterministic execution in the original program may become non-deterministic in the model representing the program. Given a statement such as if get $a := 55$ then set $b := 12$ else set $c := 4$ we cannot determine the contents of region a, and hence have to consider that the statements contained in either the true or false branches could be executed. It is likely that we will extend our dependence graph representation at some point in the future to include data-flow in a similar way to that described in [9].

We create a dependence graph for the program using the algorithm in Figure 3 for each statement s in the function. We use some notation to specify the algorithm: Let C be a stack to contain references to vertices with conventional $push_C(v)$, pop_C and top_C operations. Let t, t_{true}, t_{false} and t_{expr} be variables, each holding a reference to a vertex. We denote assignment to a variable with the := operator. t is always the last vertex to be created, t_{true}, t_{false} and t_{expr} are the last vertices of the true and false branches of a conditional statement, with t_expr the last vertex of the boolean expression that controls it. $CreateGraph(F)$ means that we create a function entry vertex v_{entry} and function exit vertex v_{exit}, and perform $push_C(v_{entry})$. CD, TR, and V stand for control dependence, transition relation, and vertex.

The graph for program P is in Figure 4. Some simplifications have been made in the graph shown in this paper (for reasons of clarity). Arguments in a Do function call are applied one at a time, returning a function value after each application to which the next argument is applied until all of the arguments have been provided. A function call with n arguments in the program will therefore produce n pairs of function call nodes in the dependency graph; for example, each of the function calls in P will be represented by 3 pairs of vertices, each with function call and return edges. Since the complexity is the result of the language rather than the model extraction technique itself, we represent function calls in the graph with a single pair of nodes.

Vertices in the graph are classified into several vertex types, with each vertex having exactly one type. The different types consist of statement, expression, function entry, function exit, function call and function return vertices. The majority of statements in the source program are translated to vertices of the

set $id := E$	get id
Create a V v labelled $\{$set id$\}$ Create a V v' labelled the effect of E. Add a CD edge from v to top_C Add a CD edge from v' to v Add a TR edge from t to v' Add a TR edge from v' to v $t := v$	Create a V v labelled $\{$get id$\}$ Add a TR edge from t to v Add a CD edge from v to top_C $t := v$

let $id := E$	return E
Create a V v labelled the effect of E. Add a CD edge from v to top_C Add a TR edge from t to v $t := v$	Create a V v labelled the effect of E. Add a CD edge from v_{exit} to v. Add a CD edge from v to top_C Add a TR edge from t to v Add a TR edge from v to v_{exit} pop_t

if E then S_{true}	if E then S_{true} else S_{false}

Create a V v labelled the empty effect
Add a CD edge from v to top_C
Add a TR edge from t to v
$push_C(v)$
$CreateGraph(E)$
$t_{expr} := t$
$CreateGraph(s_{true})$
$t_{true} := t$
If execution of S_{true} can reach
   the following statement
      Create a V v_{end}
      Create a CD edge
         from v_{end} to v
      Create TR edges from
         t_{true} to v_{end} and t_{expr} to v_{end}
      $t := v_{end}$
Otherwise
      $t := t_{expr}$
pop_C
	Create a V v labelled the empty effect
	Add a CD edge from v to top_C
	Add a TR edge from t to v
	$push_C(v)$
	$CreateGraph(E)$
	$t_{expr} := t$
	$CreateGraph(s_{true})$
	$t_{true} := t$
	$CreateGraph(s_{false})$
	$t_{false} := t$
	If execution of both s_{true} and s_{false}
	   can reach the following statement
	      Create a V v_{end}
	      Create a CD edge from
	         v_{end} to v
	      Create TR edges from
	         t_{true} to v_{end} and t_{false} to v_{end}
	      $t := v_{end}$
	Otherwise, if execution of only s_{true}
	   can reach the following statement
	      $t := s_{true}$
	Otherwise $t := s_{false}$
	$pop_C(v)$

id $params$			
Omitted for space reasons			

E_1 bop E_2	uop E	S_1 ; S_2	
$CreateGraph(E_1)$ $CreateGraph(E_2)$	$CreateGraph(E)$	$CreateGraph(S_1)$ $CreateGraph(S_2)$	

Fig. 3. Graph Extraction Algorithm

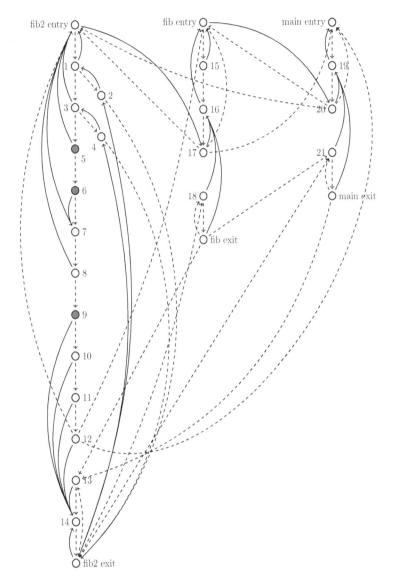

Fig. 4. Graph for Program P With Vertices Selected On First Stage of Slicing with Criterion *get* < *a* >

statement vertex type, which are labelled with the effect performed by the statement. The function entry and function exit vertices do not directly correspond to statements in the program: they are created as entry and exit points for the subset of the control flow graph corresponding to a particular function definition. Likewise, function call and function return vertices are created at function call sites to indicate the transfer of execution to and from another function.

Edges in the control-flow graph are classified in a similar manner to vertices, with 4 different edge types: control dependency edges, transition edges, function call and function call return edges.

We do not create nodes for region declaration, dependency declaration or thread creation statements, as regions, dependencies and threads exist throughout the entire life of the program and such statements cannot appear inside functions.

To enable the creation of control-dependence edges during the creation of the graph the last function entry or conditional statement vertex is tracked using a stack, and control dependence edges are generated during the creation of each new vertex by adding an edge to the vertex at the top of the stack. The transition relation is generated by keeping track of the last generated vertex to enable a transition edge to be added when a new vertex is created.

6   Slicing

Once the graph representation of program behaviour has been created we select a subset of the vertices in the graph called a *slice*. The slice is created with regard to a *slicing criterion* to obtain a subgraph containing only vertices with effects specified in the slicing criterion and vertices representing control flow statements.

Our slicing criterion and method differ from that described in [16] and [9] in some important respects. In existing approaches to program slicing, the slicing criterion consists of a variable x at a particular point in the program and produces a subprogram consisting of all statements that are involved in the computation of the value of x or can be affected by the x (depending upon whether forward or backward slicing is being performed). In contrast, we use a set of effects $\Sigma = \{\sigma_1, .. \sigma_n\}$ as the slicing criterion. Given a dependence graph g, we produce a subgraph g' containing only vertices labelled with instances of effects in $\Sigma \cup Dep(\sigma_1) \cup Dep(\sigma_2) \cup ... \cup Dep(\sigma_n)$ from the entire program. The sliced graph for program P is in Figure 5.

In doing so, we produce a slice that includes all instances of the specified behaviour from the entire program, and the effects of other statements (such as conditional statements and function calls) required for these effects and execution paths to be performed. The dependency relationships between effects are important here as they enable us to create a model that includes not only the behaviours specified in the slicing criterion but also behaviours that may influence the outcome of those in the slicing criterion and therefore must also be included. The dependency relationships bet-weens effects are important here, as

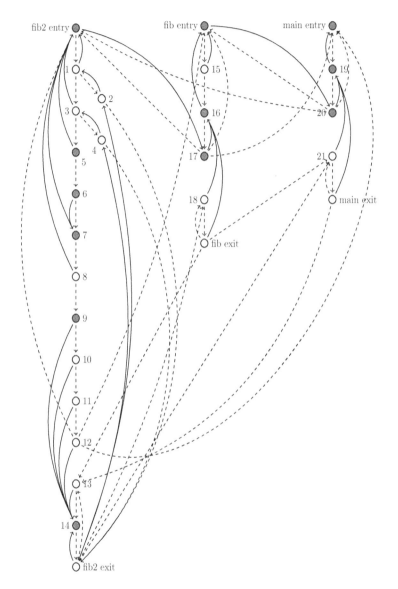

Fig. 5. Graph for P Sliced With Criterion $get < a >$

they enable us to create a model that includes not only the behaviours specified in the slicing criterion but also behaviours that may influence the outcome of those in the slicing criterion and therefore must also be included.

We utilise a breadth-first node-marking approach, in which vertices with effects that unify with some element in our slicing criterion or its dependencies are first marked and added to a queue. The nodes marked in this step are shown in Figure 4. The vertex v at the head of the queue is then removed, and all unmarked vertices immediately reachable from v via control dependency edges are also marked and added to the back of the queue. The process is repeated until the queue is empty, at which point the slice consists of the marked subgraph.

7 Model Extraction through a LTS

Once a subgraph of the graph from Section 5 has been created, we produce a labelled transition system in the form of a stack automaton from which the final PROMELA model is created. Each vertex v with label σ in the control flow graph becomes a transition t labelled with σ between states in the automaton.

The stack in the automaton provides the ability to return to the appropriate state after reaching the end of the states representing a function. Function call and function exit vertices in the graph become transitions states at which the stack must be manipulated or used to determine the next state in the model.

We denote transitions in the automaton with a quintuple (s_1, s_2, σ, w, r) where s_1 and s_2 are the start and end states of the transition, σ is an effect, r is the identifier of a state to be read from the top of the stack and w the identifier of a state to push onto the stack (with λ indicating that nothing is to be read from the stack or popped onto the stack). We assume that values read from the stack are removed.

We indicate a transition edge between vertices v and v' in the graph as $(v, v')_T$, a control dependence edge between v and v' as $(v, v')_D$, a function call edge between v and v' as $(v, v')_F$ and a function call return edge between v and v' as $(v, v')_R$.

We create the automaton as follows: Let L be a stack to contain references to states with conventional $push_L(s)$, pop_L and top_L operations. Let E be a stack to contain references to states with conventional $push_E(s)$, pop_E and top_E operations. Let V be a list to contain visited vertices. Then proceed by applying these steps

- $M := \emptyset$
- Create a start state S_{start} and end state S_{end}
- Create start and end states for the main function $S_{mainstart}$ and $S_{mainend}$
- Add transitions $(S_{start}, S_{mainstart}, empty, S_{end}, \lambda)$
  and $(S_{mainend}, S_{end}, empty, \lambda, S_{end})$
- $push_L(S_{start})$
- If there is no v in the input graph such that $(v_{start}, v)_T$
  add a new transition $(S_{start}, S_{end}, empty, \lambda, \lambda)$ to the automaton and finish.

- Otherwise $process(S_{mainstart})$
- pop_L

together with $process(v)$ appearing in Figure 6. The automaton for P is in Figure 7.

It is relatively simple to create a representation of the program from the automaton in the PROMELA input language of the Spin model checker. We use a two-stage process. In the initial stage, the input program is read to build lists of the regions, processes and effects from the top-level declarations. A standard PROMELA program outline is used for elements common to all models of Do programs such as the declaration of the process stack and stack pointer, current state and last action variables. In the second phase, the automaton created from the sliced program is used to generate the states of the model. Each state in the automaton is numbered, and the behaviour of the model is produced by a PROMELA do statement indexed by the current state number. Transitions between states in the automaton become assignments to the currentstate variable in the model, and the lasteffect variable is used to record the effect label of the last transition made by the model checker to bring it into the current state. For reasons of space we omit the model for P from this paper.

8 Conclusions and Future Work

In this paper we have presented a method of creating simple models of program behaviour from programs in a language with an effect system.

It would be possible to extend our models to include system state such as the contents of memory regions rather than simply produce traces of effects that occur. Such an approach would allow execution in the source program that at present becomes non-deterministic in the generated model to be represented in a deterministic manner, and therefore remove traces in the model that do not correspond to possible execution paths in the program. Our graph representation and slicing algorithm would have to be extended to consider data-flow as well as control-flow in the original program, and we would need to consider additional types of effect dependencies. For instance, when an expression appearing in the condition of a conditional statement has an effect, we would need to include that effect and its dependencies in the model to properly evaluate the conditional statement. From the preliminary work undertaken here, we believe that such extensions will be a considerable undertaking.

The automata and models produced by the method detailed in this paper are certainly not minimal, so it would be possible to modify our algorithms to produce fewer states and empty transitions or add an additional minimisation stage before generating the final PROMELA model.

The Do language has a limited syntax and set of primitive effects. We intend to extend the language with further control statements and additional effects such as thread synchronisation and mutual exclusion, which would make the system significantly more useful for verifying concurrent programs.

$process(v) =$
Let $S_{funstart}$ and S_{funend} be the start and end states of the function containing v.
For each vertex v:

Function entry vertex:
- If v is marked and $v \notin V$
  * $push_L(S_{funstart})$
  * $V := V \cup \{v\}$
  * For every v' such that there exists a transition edge $(v, v')_T$ in the input graph $process(v')$
  * pop_L

Function exit vertex:
- Add a new transition $(top_L, S_{funend}, empty, \lambda, \lambda)$.
- $M := M \cup \{(v, top_L, S_{funend})\}$
- $V := V \cup \{v\}$

Function call vertex:
- If v is marked
  * Add a function call return state S_{return}
  * $V := V \cup \{v\}$
  * Add a transition $(top_L, s_{return}, empty, \lambda, \lambda)$
  * $push_L(s_{return})$
  * For every v' such that there exists a transition edge $(v, v')_T$ in the input graph $process(v')$
- For every marked vertex v'' such that there exists a function call edge $(v, v'')_F$ in the graph:
  * Create a transition $(top_L, v''_{funstart}, empty, \lambda, S_{return})$ where $v''_{funstart}$ is the start state of the function containing v''
  * $process(v'')$
  * Create a transition $(v''_{funend}, S_{return}, empty, S_{return}, \lambda)$ where v''_{funend} is the end state of the function containing v''
- pop_L

Function call return vertex:
- For every v' such that (v, v') is a transition edge in the graph:
  * If $(v', s, s') \notin M$ or $v' \neq top_L$ then $process(v')$
  * Otherwise add a transition $(top_L, s, empty, \lambda, \lambda)$ where $(v', s, s') \in M$

Other vertex types:
- If v is marked, $v \notin V$ and v has a non-empty effect:
  * Add a new state s
  * Add a new transition $(top_L, s, Eff(v), \lambda, \lambda)$
  * $V := V \cup \{v\}$
  * $M := M \cup (v, top_L, s)$
  * $push_L(s)$
  * $pushed := true$
- If $(v, s', s'') \notin M$ or $s'' \neq top_L$ then $process(v')$
- Otherwise add a transition $(top_L, s', empty, \lambda, \lambda)$
- If $pushed = true$ then pop_L

Fig. 6. Automaton Algorithm

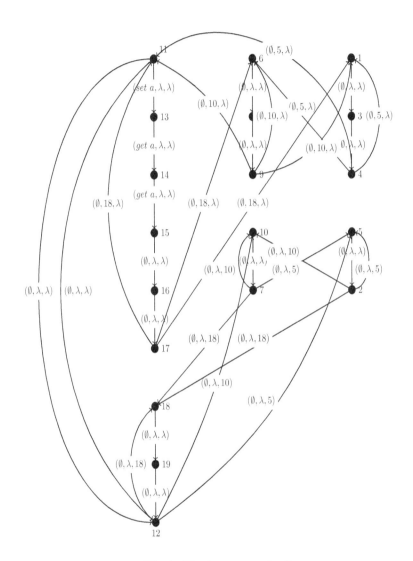

Fig. 7. The Automaton for P

41

Do has a formal operational semantics, but our work so far has not led to the formalization of the algorithms described and implemented here. Clearly a more complete formalization together with proofs of mutual correctness would be most desirable, and we plan to consider this in due course.

References

1. Andrew W. Appel and Jens Palsberg. *Modern Compiler Implementation in Java*. Cambridge University Press, 2003.
2. Timo Bingmann. Flex bison c++ template/example 0.1.4. http://idlebox.net/2007/flex-bison-cpp-example/.
3. Bison manual. http://www.gnu.org/software/bison/manual/.
4. R. L. Crole. Operational Semantics, Abstract Machines and Correctness, 2008. Lecture Notes for the Midlands Graduate School in the Foundations of Computer Science, LATEX format 91 pages with subject and notation index, plus slides 1-up and 8-up.
5. R. L. Crole and A. D. Gordon. Relating Operational and Denotational Semantics for Input/Output Effects. *Mathematical Structures in Computer Science*, 9:125–158, 1999.
6. M. Felleisen and D. Friedman. *Control Operators, the SECD-machine, and the λ-calculus*, pages 193–217. North Holland, 1986.
7. Lexical analysis with flex. http://flex.sourceforge.net/manual/.
8. J. Hatcliff, M.B. Dwyer, and H. Zheng. Slicing software for model construction. *Higher-order and Symbolic Computation*, 13:315–353, 2000.
9. Susan Horwitz, Thomas Reps, and David Binkley. Interprocedural slicing using dependence graphs. *ACM Transations on Programming Languages and Systems*, 12:26—60, 1990.
10. Michael Huth and Mark Ryan. *Logic in Computer Science: Modelling and Reasoning About Systems*. Cambridge University Press, Cambridge [U.K.], 2nd ed edition, 2004.
11. J. M. Lucassen and D. K. Gifford. Polymorphic effect systems. In *Proceedings of the 15th ACM SIGPLAN-SIGACT symposium on Principles of programming languages*, pages 47–57, San Diego, California, United States, 1988. ACM.
12. Daniel Marino and Todd Millstein. A generic type-and-effect system. In *Proceedings of the 4th international workshop on Types in language design and implementation*, pages 39–50, Savannah, GA, USA, 2009. ACM.
13. Eugenio Moggi. Computational Lambda-Calculus and monads. *Information and Computation*, pages 14—23, 1988.
14. Steven S. Muchnick. *Advanced compiler design and implementation*. Morgan Kaufmann Publishers Inc., 1997.
15. Philip Wadler and Peter Thiemann. The marriage of effects and monads. *ACM Trans. Comput. Logic*, 4(1):1–32, 2003.
16. J. Zhao. Multithreaded dependence graphs for concurrent java programs. In *Software Engineering for Parallel and Distributed Systems, 1999. Proceedings. International Symposium on*, pages 13–23, 1999.

Augmenting Authoring of Adaptation Languages via Visual Environments

Jan D. Bothma and Alexandra I. Cristea

Department of Computer Science, University of Warwick, Coventry, CV4 7AL
{J.D.Bothma, A.I.Cristea}@warwick.ac.uk

Abstract. Adaptive Educational Hypermedia (AEH) ideally allows for the delivery of the right information to the right student. Strategies for adaptation can be described via the LAG language. The PEAL tool offers many common programming environment features to ease development in LAG but authoring adaptation strategies is still considered time-consuming and difficult, especially for the inexperienced author. Visual Programming Environments have been shown to ease entry to programming for a new platform for beginner and experienced programmers. In this paper we ease entry to adaptation strategy authoring by providing a visual environment for creating strategies alongside the text-based programming environment of PEAL which propagates changes from either representation to the other. This allows the lay person author to create adaptation strategies with little experience of programming or the LAG language while becoming familiar with LAG at their own pace, thus lowering the threshold for authoring in the complex environment of Adaptive Hypermedia.

Keywords: Adaptive Hypermedia, Visual Programming, LAG

1 Introduction

Adaptive Hypermedia (AH) [7] adapts content for any given user according to what is called the *User Model*. This stores information about a particular user to adapt to their needs such as their knowledge level, interests, goals, preferred learning styles, situational parameters, etc., and thus delivers information that is appropriate to them. The LAOS Framework [12] separates the different aspects of Adaptive Hypermedia into the Domain, Goal and Constraints, User, Adaptation and Presentation Models.

There are currently few tools that deliver adaptive hypermedia, and even fewer that provide authoring support. My Online Teacher (MOT)[14] is one of the only tools to provide a generic platform for authoring and reusing adaptive educational hypermedia. It is supported by two export formats. The *Common Adaptation Format* (CAF) [14] stores the static content which makes up the relevant content of the Domain Model, and the lesson structure in the Goal and Constraints Model. The *LAG language* [13] implements the Adaptation Model. These formats offer a compact way of storing and exchanging adaptive hypermedia information between systems and together allow a compatible Adaptation

Engine to provide an online lesson which adapts to users according to their User Model.

In this paper we describe the research towards improving the authoring process for adaptive hypermedia. This includes improving the authoring tools that can deploy the following main methods:

- Help and support tools
- Function distance[1]
- (Semi-)automating the authoring process[2]
- Visualisation of authoring steps

Here we are describing the design and implementation of a tool aimed at weak (beginner) programmers and non-programmers which aims to help them be able to create relatively complex adaptation strategies for web presentations. Thus, we aim to lower the threshold for the lay person in creating personalization and adaptation scenarios. For this purpose, we aim specifically at one of the most challenging areas of improvement – that of visualization of the authoring steps. We will focus specifically on creating visualizations of the adaptation behaviour description, and not the more straightforward (and more commonly seen) content description.

As the MOT tool already presents a developed environment for generic authoring, as well as a language set for both content and adaptation specification, the current visualization improvements as proposed in this paper are based on the MOT tool. Thus the tool presented here is a visual representation of and equivalent to the LAG adaptation language; directly based on its grammar and semantics. It does not attempt to develop a new adaptation programming paradigm, as is being undertaken by the GRAPPLE project [15].

The remainder of this paper is organized as follows: Sect. 2 discusses the problem description; Sect. 3 explains the background to this project and related work; Sect. 4 describes the development and implementation of our solution; Sect. 5 documents our evaluation of the solution and Sect. 6 concludes with our findings.

2 Problem Description

A recently-completed dedicated LAG editor, the Programming Environment for Adaptation Language (PEAL) has been evaluated by Cristea et. al [13] where a sample of the target users of this editor, experienced programmers, unanimously agreed that it was better for authoring in the LAG language than the existing text editing tools. However, non-programmers and programmers new to LAG and the MOT system can still find programming in the LAG language intimidating. Cristea et al. noted in [13] that the existing strategy creation tool in MOT is

---

[1] Clicks needed to perform an action from a given state
[2] e.g. automatic content generation, automatic link generation, etc.

out of date, and that a visual tool for developing strategies is desired to lower the threshold for authoring in the LAG language.

It is important for the authoring environment to be online [13]. A web-based authoring environment offers wide availability and eases collaboration. PEAL is a web-based programming environment and has several valuable features which can be built upon to achieve our goals. This includes online private and shared storage of adaptation strategies which allows collaboration and reuse, meaning authors do not have to start with completely blank strategies but can work from an example. The use of PEAL's LAG parser for converting adaptation strategies to our visual representation is discussed in Sect. 4.

The highest level of the LAG Framework [11] is the 'Adaptation Strategy'. LAG strategies have a plain text description which allows authors to (re-)use existing strategies without needing any knowledge of LAG. Unfortunately these descriptions are rarely verbose enough, when written at all, to allow reuse by the lay author. It is therefore important to make writing the description an integral part of the authoring process and as easy and informative as possible.

3 Background

The field of Visual Programming Environments is heavily researched [16]. Like parser generators, visual programming environment generators are available [6, 10]. Unfortunately the formats of these outputs are difficult to port to the strict web browser-based format desired for this project. This means that even if a useful visual environment for LAG could be produced by such an automated tool, significant effort would be required to port the result to the web browser.

The LAG creation tool which exists within MOT is out of date in terms of LAG grammar [13]. It is also based on older website interaction methods which require reloading the page to update content. JavaScript engines in web browsers have improved significantly since the MOT tool was implemented, offering efficient and intuitive interactive application capabilities within web browsers.

The Adobe Flash [1] plug-in used by the GRAPPLE project and Java Applets used by AHA! are often used for rich interactive online applications. However, the advances in web technologies mean that similarly rich and efficient interfaces can now be created without plug-ins, offering capable applications with minimal software requirements.

Casella et. al [8] define a collection of visual languages implemented in the SEAMAN tool which allow authoring of adaptive e-learning courses. A recent assessment of their usability [9] shows encouraging results for the application of visual environments to adaptive e-learning course authoring. However, this system only updates the User Model based on a student's performance in tests following lessons. LAG, on the other hand, allows direct manipulation of the User Model and Presentation Model every time the user accesses a concept. This allows the adaptation of the next concept visited by the user based on the last concept they visited within the current lesson. While adaptive courses generated using the SEAMAN tool could potentially be converted to the common platform provided by MOT, we would like to maintain the expressivity of LAG in our visual environment. The SEAMAN tool is therefore not suitable for our requirements.

4 The PEAL 2 Visual Programming Environment

We followed a strategy of developing a basic working visual environment while integrating semantics and visual feedback of the programming domain of adaptation strategies in parallel.

4.1 The Visual Environment

Visual elements have been implemented to represent each LAG language construct. Where a construct can contain other constructs or code such as a list of statements or operands to an operator, a visual element container holds child elements which make up the complete element. Strategies can be created using the visual environment by inserting elements into appropriate containers. Visual elements can be dragged to other containers by clicking and dragging the element with a mouse.

To give an example of a visual element, Fig. 1 shows a screenshot of the *Each-Concept Condition-Action* visual element implemented in PEAL 2. This visual element represents the LAG *while* construct which can be seen with an additional comparison and statement in Listing 1. The effect of the *while* construct is to execute each contained statement with respect to each *Concept* which is part of the Goal Model of the current adaptive course for which the condition is satisfied. This visual element represents that behaviour as a flowchart-like loop from a *multiple-documents* symbol labeled "For each concept in the lesson", to a *condition rhombus*, to a *process box* and back to the *multiple-documents* symbol.

The context menu[3] opened over the *process box* in Fig. 1 allows the insertion of new visual elements such as *Assignment* statements like PM.GM.Concept.show = true as shown in Listing 1. The insertion option is only available for visual element containers and depends on the context – the context menu for the *condition rhombus* condition container only allows insertion of condition visual elements which could, for example, represent the comparison in Listing 1.

```
while ( GM.Concept.weight > 5 ) (
    PM.GM.Concept.show = true
)
```

Listing 1. LAG *while* construct with a *greater-than* comparison and one assignment statement

The *Help* option, as shown in Fig. 1, displays the documentation section specifically relevant to the context. For example, in the above context, the section

---
[3] displayed upon right-click in Microsoft Windows operating systems

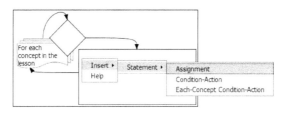

Fig. 1. PEAL 2 *Each-Concept Condition-Action* visual element with the *Insert* part of its context menu open

on *Statement List*s shown in Fig. 2 would be displayed, since the context is a container for a list of *Statement* visual elements. A single user documentation web page was created which can be read as a whole like traditional documentation. Each topic was, however, given a distinct name using the HTML *id* attribute like *statement-list-documentation-section* in the above example. JavaScript embedded in the documentation then collapses each section to show only its title, except for the chosen section which is displayed fully. Following cross-referencing links in the documentation expands those sections. This shows the user only the relevant information to avoid information overload but gives them the freedom to explore more topics easily.

- Editor overview
- Quick tips
- Visual Element Features
  - Attribute container
  - Value container
  - Condition container
  - Statement list

  A Statement List can have multiple statements. Statements can be re-ordered by dragging

  See also:
  Initialization tab
  Implementation tab
  Condition-Action visual element
  Each-Concept Condition-Action visual element
  Assignment visual element

Fig. 2. Screenshot of contextual documentation opened using the context menu in Fig. 1

We have also made use of *tooltips* which are very brief descriptions that can be used to identify visual elements and their parts when the mouse cursor is held over them.

Visual feedback is provided to indicate where a dragged element can validly be inserted. The containers where a visual element may be dropped are coloured

47

green while the element is held, as can be seen in Fig. 3 b and 3 c. An assignment can be dropped in the *then* and *else* parts but not in the *condition rhombus*. The container resizes to accommodate the dragged element when it is entered by the mouse cursor (Fig. 3 c). As users drag elements around the programming environment, they can thus quickly see and learn where different kinds of elements can be placed.

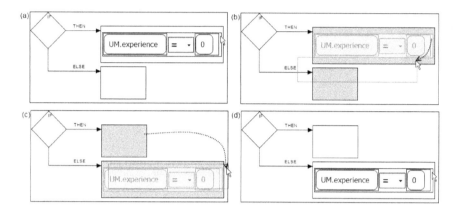

Fig. 3. Sequence of a PEAL 2 *Assignment* element in the *then* part of a *Condition-Action* visual element (**a**) which is dragged (**b-c**) to the *else* part where it is released (**d**)

The visual environment is placed on a *tab* on the PEAL 2 web application. This hides the PEAL text environment until the user changes to the text editor tab, at which point the visual representation is converted to LAG to update the text environment. Changing from the text tab to the visual tab converts the LAG language text to the visual representation to propagate changes made to the LAG code.

The strategy description is placed on a third tab. To encourage the author to write a thorough description, this tab is coloured red initially. The words are counted as the user types and the tab is changed to green once the strategy description consists of 20 words or more.

4.2 Conversion from the Visual Representation to LAG

The Object-Oriented implementation of visual elements proved to make converting the visual representation to LAG very easy. A *toLAG()* method exists for each visual element object. This returns the LAG representation of that element which wraps the LAG of its decendent elements by calling *toLAG()* on each child in its visual element containers.

4.3 Conversion from LAG to the Visual Representation

PEAL already featured a LAG parser implemented in JavaScript based on the CodeMirror framework [2]. This is used to perform syntax colouring and syntax error checking. A parser is needed in PEAL 2 to convert LAG to the visual representation. Although parser generators exist that can output JavaScript implementations, we decided not to duplicate effort by implementing and maintaining two parsers but instead to use that of PEAL for all purposes in PEAL 2.

PEAL's parser is similar to recursive descent parsers [5] in that a function exists for each nonterminal. However, instead of these functions directly making recursive calls to expand nonterminals, the functions, referred to as *actions*, representing the expected non-terminals are placed onto a stack and the current token is consumed. These *action* functions check that expected tokens are found, set token styles for syntax colouring, report syntax errors and consume tokens as appropriate.

We added more actions which create visual elements as the relevant LAG tokens are consumed. The JavaScript code in Listing 2 shows part of the function which parses LAG statements – the part for the *if-then-else* construct in particular[4]. The *ToVisual.actions.startIf* action was added to create the *Condition-Action* visual element, seen in Fig. 3, which is the PEAL 2 visual representation of the common *if-then-else* construct. To insert nested visual elements in the correct block context, a stack of visual elements represents the current position in the visual element hierarchy.

```
// Dispatches various types of statements
//   based on the type of the current token.
function statement(type, tokenValue) {
    if (type == "if") {
        cont(
            ToVisual.actions.startIf,
            condition,
            then,
            ToVisual.actions.finishIf
        );
    } else if ( type == "while" ) { // etc.
```

Listing 2. Part of JavaScript function which parses the LAG *statement* non-terminal

The correct syntax is reliably converted to the visual representation, although incorrect syntax is not yet handled in conversion but is only marked red for the user to correct by hand with the help of syntax error messages as in the original PEAL tool.

---

[4] Actions maintaining lexical scope for indentation in the PEAL editor have been removed here for simplicity

4.4 JavaScript Implementation

Each HTML element exists in the browser as a Document Object Model (DOM) [3] node. The Yahoo User Interface library (YUI) [17] provides a JavaScript object which wraps a DOM node, allowing browser-independent interaction with the DOM.

Visual elements are created entirely using JavaScript to create HTML and SVG[4] elements and are styled using Cascading Style Sheets (CSS). This means additional elements can easily be specified by adding references to extension JavaScript and CSS files to the PEAL 2 environment in the future.

5 Evaluation

We assessed whether PEAL 2 makes it easier for non-programmers to author adaptation strategies using the following evaluation:

Based on the evaluation of the PEAL tool [13], we developed a set of tasks followed by a set of questions.

Tasks

1. Author a strategy from scratch using the PEAL 2 visual environment.
2. Author a strategy from scratch using the PEAL 2 text environment.
3. Extend an existing strategy using both the visual and text editors.

Questions

1. What are the main strengths of the visual and text LAG editors?
2. What are the main weaknesses of the visual and text LAG editors?
3. Would you prefer to use the PEAL 2 visual environment, the text environment or some other editor to author strategies in LAG?
4. Other comments?

This evaluation was performed with three subjects with no programming experience and one subject with only experience of writing HTML markup. All subjects were given a short presentation explaining the LAOS framework and how adaptation strategies can be implemented in LAG. The LAG grammar and semantic definitions were provided but only a verbal explanation of the visual elements was given as the user documentation had not been prepared at the time of the evaluation.

Subjects made the following comments after using the text editor and visual environment:

1. Two subjects found the visual representation easier to understand as an adaptation process while finding the text version very abstract.
2. Two subjects found the text editor alongside the grammar and semantics more intuitive and noted that this format is more familiar to them in their degree language studies.

3. One subject recommended using colour to help distinguish different kinds of visual elements like the syntax highlighting of the text editor.
4. The meaning of some of the components of the visual representation, e.g. the flowchart condition-rhombus, had to be explained to users not familiar with them.
5. To several subjects, the effect of a strategy was evident very quickly in the visual representation once the meaning of components was clear.

Two out of the four subjects preferred the visual environment implemented in PEAL 2 over the existing PEAL text editor. When a strategy was shown in the visual environment, those subjects immediately expressed how much easier the visual representation was to follow. It was clear that a tutorial-style explanation based on examples was desired by all subjects, as well as documentation of the visual elements. For this reason, we placed a higher priority on providing user documentation which was implemented after this evaluation. The two subjects who preferred the text editor were more comfortable referring to the LAG language grammar and semantics specifications than diagrammatic representations of a strategy. This shows the value of offering the option of using the text editor even to non-programmers as done in PEAL 2.

6 Conclusion

In this paper we have documented the development of a visual environment for authoring adaptation from the design, to implementation, to the evaluation. Section 4 described how our design was implemented using the latest web technologies stable and compatible enough for wide use without dependence on third-party plugins. The structured implementation prepares the tool for further extensions. The evaluation documented in Sect. 5 shows that the visual environment described here lowers the threshold for authoring adaptation strategies for visually oriented non-programmers. By offering the visual environment alongside the existing PEAL text environment, text-oriented authors are still catered for and authors can choose the most appropriate environment as they gain experience. Furthermore, we have shown how some key areas of improvement discovered through the evaluation have been implemented to further improve the state for the lay person author.

7 Further Work

In addition to improving the current state of authoring tools, PEAL 2 can be built on in the following ways:

- Extend PEAL's code fragment storage and reuse to the visual environment
- Improve compatibility with more common web browsers
- Improve handling of bad syntax during conversion to the visual representation

- Improve syntax checking to list multiple errors
- Framework for writing and importing documentation translations
- Compare attribute references in CAF content and LAG strategies to give author an indication of whether they are compatible
- Provide direct output to adaptation delivery engines to allow immediate preview and testing of new adaptive hypermedia systems
- Use colour to provide further visual feedback and identification cues

References

1. Adobe flash platform, http://www.adobe.com/flashplatform/
2. CodeMirror: In-browser code editing made almost bearable, http://marijn.haverbeke.nl/codemirror/
3. Document Object Model (DOM) Level 3 Core Specification, http://www.w3.org/TR/DOM-Level-3-Core/
4. Scalable Vector Graphics (SVG), http://www.w3.org/Graphics/SVG/
5. Aho, A.V., Lam, M.S., Sethi, R., Ullman, J.D.: Compilers: principles, techniques, and tools. Addison-Wesley, Boston, MA, USA, 2nd edn. (2007)
6. Backlund, B., Hagsand, O., Pehrson, B.: Generation of visual language-oriented design environments. Journal of Visual Languages & Computing 1(4), 333–354 (1990)
7. Brusilovsky, P.: Adaptive hypermedia. User Modeling and User-Adapted Interaction 11(1-2), 87–110 (2001)
8. Casella, G., Costagliola, G., Ferrucci, F., Polese, G., Scanniello, G.: Visual languages for defining adaptive and collaborative e-learning activities. In: Isaas, P., Kommers, P., McPherson, M. (eds.) Proceedings of IADIS International Conference e-Society 2004. vol. 1, pp. 243–250. IADIS Press, Ávila, Spain (2004)
9. Costagliola, G., De Lucia, A., Ferrucci, F., Gravino, C., Scanniello, G.: Assessing the usability of a visual tool for the definition of e-learning processes. Journal of Visual Languages & Computing 19(6), 721–737 (2008)
10. Costagliola, G., Deufemia, V., Polese, G., Risi, M.: Building syntax-aware editors for visual languages. Journal of Visual Languages & Computing 16(6), 508–540 (2005), selected papers from Visual Languages and Formal Methods 2004 (VLFM '04)
11. Cristea, A.I., Calvi, L.: The three layers of adaptation granularity. In: Brusilovsky, P., Corbett, A.T., de Rosis, F. (eds.) User Modeling. pp. 4–14. Springer, Johnstown, PA, USA (2003)
12. Cristea, A.I., de Mooij, A.: LAOS: Layered WWW AHS Authoring Model with Algebraic Operators. In: WWW (Alternate Paper Tracks) (2003)
13. Cristea, A.I., Smits, D., Bevan, J., Hendrix, M.: LAG 2.0: Refining a Reusable Adaptation Language and Improving on Its Authoring. In: EC-TEL. pp. 7–21 (2009)
14. Cristea, A.I., Smits, D., De Bra, P.: Towards a generic adaptive hypermedia platform: a conversion case study. Journal of Digital Information 8(3) (2007)
15. Hendrix, M., De Bra, P., Pechenizkiy, M., Smits, D., Cristea, A.I.: Defining Adaptation in a Generic Multi Layer Model: CAM: The GRAPPLE Conceptual Adaptation Model. In: Dillenbourg, P., Specht, M. (eds.) EC-TEL. LNCS, vol. 5192, pp. 132–143. Springer (2008)

16. Nickerson, J.V.: Visual programming. Ph.D. thesis, New York University, New York, NY, USA (1995)
17. YUI 3 – Yahoo! User Interface Library, http://developer.yahoo.com/yui/3/

Towards Rendering Optical Phenomena

Max A Rady and Richard E Overill
Department of Computer Science, King's College London
Strand, London, WC2R 2LS, UK
{max.rady, richard.overill}@kcl.ac.uk

Abstract. The paper focuses on creating vivid, realistic, and eye-pleasing imagery with the ultimate goal of rendering phenomena, such as rainbows, halos, and glories. To the authors' knowledge this has not yet been attempted. In addition, it is an interesting break away from the traditional use of small indoor scenes with exact world scene setups for global illumination and instead attempting to recreate fascinating optical phenomena which were only beginning to fo be fully understood in the seventeenth century by Descartes and Newton.

Keywords: Path Tracing, Photon Mapping, Optical Phenomena

1 Introduction and Background

Global illumination is a set of methods which deal with the reproduction of applying lighting to a scene and then dealing with the interaction of the light with the scene in all of the various models that are associated with light. A key notion to keep in mind is that almost none of these methods are a complete solution for replicating how light behaves in the real world, and as such, it is usual in real world practice to use some sort of combination of these methods to overcome the weaknesses of the methods individually. With such information in mind, after examination of all the methods available, it was determined that the two methods that should be used to achieve the goals of this research are path tracing and photon mapping. Path tracing is a depth recursion brute force method of simulating the properties and behaviour of light by projecting rays from the light and the view point simultaneously, thus dealing with both direct and indirect illumination as well as naturally producing effects created by light which normally have to be implemented via special conditional checks and added functions. Effects produced naturally through path tracing include soft shadowing, caustics, depth of field, motion blur, ambient occlusion, as well as being unbiased in design. Photon mapping is a method with the ability to accurately deal with the interaction of light with materials such as glass, water, and crystals. In addition, photon mapping can deal with subsurface scattering, allowing it to mimic particulate matter in the air, thus allowing for a more realistic representation of the sky space. Another favourable feature of photon mapping is the ability to deal with spectral rendering in a much shorter render time, less noise, and fewer samples per pixel required as compared to path tracing. After implementing the previously mentioned methods one could use the following guidlines for generating the images:

- Direct illumination is handled by using the path tracer.
- Indirect illumination is also handled by the path tracer with irradiance computed using photon mapping.
- Caustics are handled by the photon mapping, to allow quick calculation even with high detail inputs.

Finally, a method of creating even more realistic imagery is using photon relaxation as carried out by Spencer at the University of Swansea [1], which improves caustics generated by light interacting with dielectric materials.

2 Theory and Concepts

Bidirectional distribution functions are the core module of the ray tracer describing how light behaves with surfaces in a mathematical way. This in turn has the material of that surface apply its attributes onto the result to produce realistic light interaction. The bidirectional distribution functions come in two main forms: reflectance (BRDF) and transmittance (BTDF), which deal, with reflective scattering of light and transmission scattering of light respectively. The renderer provided has taken the standard approach of implementing both BRDF and BTDF as super classes with their specialized derivations as noted below.

2.1 Reflectance

The BRDF, in general physics form, is defined as follows (also see Figure 1) [2]:

> **a four-dimensional function that defines how light is reflected at an opaque surface. The function takes an incoming light direction, ω_i, and outgoing direction, ω_o, both defined with respect to the surface normal n, and returns the ratio of reflected radiance exiting along ω_i to the irradiance incident on the surface from direction ω_i. Note that each direction ω is itself parameterized by azimuth angle φ and zenith angle ϑ, therefore the BRDF as a whole is 4-dimensional.**

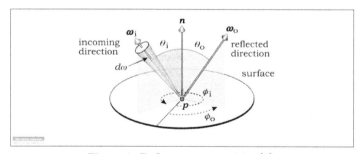

Figure 1. Reflectance quantities [3].

The equation matching the above definition is as follows, with f_r representing the BRDF, and L_r and L_i representing reflected and incident light respectively, as colours and intensities at the current stage of calculation [3]:

$$f_r(\omega_i, \omega_o) = \frac{dL_r(\omega_o)}{L_i(\omega_i)\cos(\theta_i)d\omega_i}$$

Such a definition serves well as an underlying minimum of what a BRDF must do, but the BRDF must deal with more than just opaque surfaces. Listed below are attributes with matching final physics equations of what the BRDF in the ray tracer accounts for:

- Spatial variance and invariance: BRDFs may either vary over an object surface, as a result of any number of factors, or may remain constant over an object surface. A spatial variant BRDF takes into account the factors for variation and provides an output indicative of such variation and is identified by having a hit point p parameter, while spatial invariant BRDFs do not take any variation into account [3].

$$f_r(p, \omega_i, \omega_o) = \frac{dL_r(p, \omega_o)}{L_i(p, \omega_i)\cos(\theta_i)d\omega_i}$$

- Reciprocity: allows the ray tracer to swap values ω_i with ω_o without changing the value of BRDF, formally defined as follows [3]:

$$f_r(p, \omega_i, \omega_o) = f_r(p, \omega_o, \omega_i)$$

While this may seem somewhat simple, it is actually quite an important aspect of BRDF based ray tracers as it allows the reflected radiance to stay the same, regardless of the direction it originates from.
- Linearity: a property that allows multiple BRDFs to be used to model a reflective property accurately and sum the results for that hit point p to achieve the final reflected radiance.
- Reflectance: defined as the ratio of reflected flux to incident flux.
- Perfect diffusion: the unrealistic property that light is scattered equally in all directions upon hitting a surface, which was implemented as a way of maintaining non biased abilities, and as a testing stage for the implementation of the BRDF.

2.2 Transmittance

Bidirectional transmittance distribution functions, is the shading model which describes the properties of light propagating through transparent materials upon light hitting the surface of such materials. BTDFs are a compliment of the BRDF shading techniques, but when discussing transparent materials both are essential. In addition, it should be noted that with the implementation of BTDFs a depth recursion must be implemented as some transparent materials may reflect rays for periods that are unreasonable or infinitely. The direct result of recursion depth and it's upper bound is that a ray tree is formed for each incident ray that intersects a transparent material, with the incident ray as the root and reflected and transmitted rays as left and right branches respectively, until the maximum depth is reached if the rays have not all terminated already. The ray tree can have at most $2^{max\_depth+1}$ secondary rays which can lead to extremely long rendering times if max depth is not appropriately set, but it also has a lower bound of two as it takes at least two bounces for a transmitted ray to come out of a transparent object. As a final note on ray trees it should be mentioned that the traversal method on ray trees is depth–first, with left-to-right ordering and there exist three types of ray that can occur: reflection, transmittance, and shadow (see Figure 2).

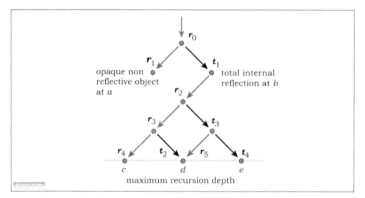

Figure 2. Example of a ray tree tracing reflectance and transmission [3].

The equations for BTDF are considerably shorter, but more complex to deal with. They are listed below with their explanation.

– First, a base equation describing exitant radiance for a transparent material which takes into account both direct and indirect illumination needs to be defined as [3]:

$$L_r(p, \omega_o) = L_{direct}(p, \omega_o) + L_{indirect}(p, \omega_o)$$

This is a straight forward and logical equation which sums the two values of radiance that are applied to a hit point p by direct and indirect illumination.
– Furthermore, indirect radiance can be described by two components which are reflected and transmitted. The equation representation is [3]:

$$L_r(p, \omega_o) = \int_{2\pi^+} f_r(p, \omega_i, \omega_o) L_i(r_c(p, \omega_i), -\omega_i) \cos(\theta_i) d\omega_i$$

where $(r_c(p, \omega_i), -\omega_i)$ is the ray casting to the nearest hit point along the ray with direction ω_i.

– Following the linearity rule it can be concluded that (see Figure 3) [3]:

$$L_i(r_c(p, \omega_i), -\omega_i) = L_o(r_c(p, \omega_i), -\omega_i)$$

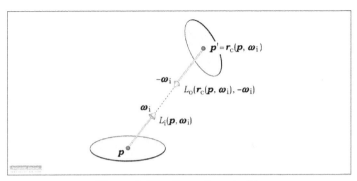

Figure 3. The linearity rule [3].

– In addition [3]:

$$L_o(r_c(p, \omega_i), -\omega_i) = L_e(p, \omega_o) + \int_{2\pi^+} f_r(p, \omega_i, \omega_o) L_o(r_c(p, \omega_i), -\omega_i) \cos(\theta_i) d\omega_i$$

In the equation immediately above there are several key definitions and issues to note, which will be discussed from left to right. First, the L_e term signifies an emissive surface, meaning a surface that is itself luminous such as the "surface" of a light. Therefore $L_e(p, \omega_o)$ is compensation for the emitted radiance in the direction ω_o. The equation for f_r is unchanged from before, leaving only exitant radiance,L_o, as the only unknown. This is an issue, as L_o is the term the equation is solving for. Such equations are known as Fredholm integral equations of the second kind and are defined as an integral based equation with constant integration limits and an unknown that appears on both sides of the equation. To make matters more complicated is the fact that L_o is recursive in nature, and only reaches a point of actual value return when cases 1, 2, or 3 of the following have been met when tracing a reflected ray [3]:

1. If the reflected ray hits no objects in the scene, return the background colour to p, where p is the point prior in the recursion call.
2. If the reflected ray hits a light source, then it returns the value for the $L_e(p, \omega_o)$ component of the equation.
3. If the reflected ray hits a point p' which is located on a non-reflective surface then direct illumination computation can be used to determine p' and return that value to p.
4. If the reflected ray hits a point p' which is located on a reflective surface it can direct illumination computation can be used to determine p', and the reflected ray, $r_{depth+1}$, is traced if the condition of current $depth + 1$ does not violate the max depth condition. Ray $r_{depth+1}$ will then return a radiance value that is added to the direct illumination value, with the combined radiance being returned to hit point p'.

This completes the reflection tracing for BRDFs entirely, and solves the reflection component for the BTDF equation discussed before, leaving only the transmittance portion to be defined and solved, as follows [3]:

$$L_t(p, \omega_o) = \int_{2\pi^-} f_t(p, \omega_i, \omega_o) L_o(r_c(p, \omega_i), -\omega_i) |\cos(\theta_i)| \, d\omega_i$$

This equation does not take into account Snell's law and the effect it has on transmitted radiance, to do so a coefficient needs to represent what fraction of computed value is lost via crossing the air-transparent barrier or vice versa. In addition, there is a coefficient of the same nature for reflective materials defining just how much of the computed reflection or transmission is lost. The equation for both involving their respective coefficient k_{type} are shown below, and are both bound to $k_{type} \in [0, 1]$ [3].

$$Reflective : L_{indirect} = k_r c_r L_i(p, \omega_i)$$

$$Trasparent : L_t = k_t \left(\frac{\eta_t^2}{\eta_i^2} \right) L_i$$

For both reflective and transparent materials the coefficients are simply applied in some manner to L_i, although there is a more detailed model for the reflective method, the main premise remains the same but a $\cos(\theta_i)$ value is introduced to allow for dealing with various special cases relating to incidence direction. In addition the c_r value is simply the colour value of the reflective material. Finally, for transmittance an addition of a simple method is needed to deal with the index of refraction of the two mediums involved along with the coefficient for transmittance. The above model for transparent materials leaves much to be desired, however, as it only offers simple transparency properties, which in the scope of this research are of little use as one must account for the advanced aspects of transparent materials, resulting in the need for true handling of dielectric materials such as the fact that k_r and k_t are dynamic as opposed to static based on the incident angle θ_i. This leads to the use of Fresnel equations, named after Augustin-Jean Fresnel which deal with the crossing of boundaries between two dielectric materials. The equations Fresnel derived deal with both parallel and perpendicular polarized light and give us the following reflectance values respectively [3]:

$$r_\| = \frac{\eta \cos(\theta_i) - \cos(\theta_t)}{\eta \cos(\theta_i) + \cos(\theta_t)}$$

$$r_\perp = \frac{\cos(\theta_i) - \eta \cos(\theta_t)}{\cos(\theta_i) + \eta \cos(\theta_t)}$$

$$\eta = \frac{\eta_{in}}{\eta_{out}}$$

To cope with these new changes a new set of values for k_r and k_t must be derived to take into account the conservation of energy resulting in the following formulae [3]:

$$k_r = \frac{1}{2}(r_\|^2 + r_\perp^2)$$

60

$$k_t = 1 - k_r$$

Two other factors must be taken into account which are normal incidence and grazing incidence angles where normal incidence angle is defined as $\theta_i = \theta_t = 0$ and grazing incidence is defined as $\theta_i = \frac{\pi}{2}$ which require no new equation derivations. These are just simply special cases worth defining that are simply applied to the two sets of Fresnel equations provided earlier. Attenuation is the final addition to realistically describing how light behaves when interacting with transparent objects and is given by the Lambert–Beer law which is defined as [4]:

$$I = I_o e^{-\mu l}$$

where I_o is the initial intesity of the light ray, l is the total distance travelled inside the medium, and

$$\mu = \frac{4\pi k}{\lambda}$$

Here, k is the refractive index of the medium that is being intersected by the light, and λ is the wavelength of the light. The Lambert–Beer law is an essential part of this research as it will allow the soft transition of light as opposed to producing extremely sharp colour bands which would be aesthetically unpleasing, and is straightforward to implement given the structure of the renderer up to this point. The formula converted to meet the renderer's variables can be derived to yield the following formulae [3]:

$$\frac{dL}{L} = -\sigma dx$$

$$L(d) = L_o e^{-\sigma d}$$

In this derivation σ is the attenuation coefficient equivalent to μ, and d is the depth recursion of the tracer, this allows radiance to decrease exponentially with distance travelled and can further reduced to a function of colour, as such [3]:

$$L(d) = c_f^d L_o$$

$$c_f = e^{-\sigma}$$

Note that c is the colour value bounded by $c \in [0, 1]$, that $c = 0$ defines black, and that $c = 1$ defines white as per normal computer based RGB convention. With a $c = 1$ there will be no filtering applied regardless of values presented for d, representing the total distance travelled within a dielectric material.

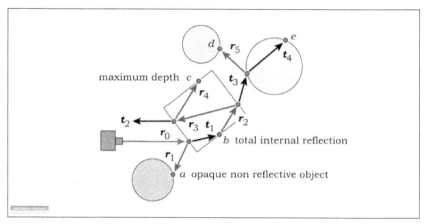

Figure 4. BRDF and BTDF actions [3].

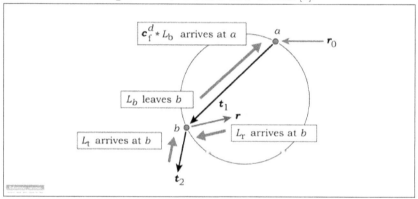

Figure 5. Lambert-Beer law visualised [3].

3 Specification, Design, and Implementation

The final version of the renderer has been designed to allow the user to specify the viewpoint, the number and size of droplets, the refractive index, the anti-solar point, the pixel resolution and the depth recursion for the number of internal reflections required. The overall system design consists of a number of modules including a ray caster, ray tracer, path tracer, and photon mapper. Ray casting doesn't allow very much sophistication to be added to the image rendered. The render does implement a ray casting tracer and whitted ray tracer as building blocks for the path tracer, and in the future the photon mapper. In reference to another path tracer that is quite minimal in design, Table 1 serves to show the variation of the same path tracer in nine different languages by comparing three metrics. The metrics used for comparison are number of lines of code, size of code relative to C++, and speed relative to C++.

Language	Size (number of lines)	Size (relative to C++)	Speed (relative to C++)
Scala 2.7.7	431	0.45	1/2.7
OCaml 3.11.0	457	0.48	1/2.3
Python 2.5.1	490	0.52	1/180
Python Shed-Skin 0.1.1	496	0.52	1/1.8
Ruby 1.8.6	498	0.52	1/218
Lua 5.1.4	568	0.60	1/52
LuaJIT 2.0.0 beta 3	568	0.60	1/13
C# 3.5	630	0.66	1/(1-5?)
Flex 2/AS3 (Flash 10.0.22.87)	644	0.68	1/55
C++ ISO-98 (LLVM-G++-4.2)	952	1.00	1
C ISO-90 (LLVM-GCC-4.2)	1197	1.26	2.1

Table 1.

Variation of a path tracer applied in 9 different languages [5].

4   Results and Discussion

The authors have noted observations of areas where improvement is required. The primary improvement is using regular grids and bounding boxes or a kd-tree structure. These can make a difference in the render times for a scene of 400×400 pixels on a 450 MHz G3 Macintosh with 512 MB RAM comparing the same ray tracer using exhaustive and regular methods shown in Table 2.

Number of Spheres	Render Times with Grid (seconds)	Render Times without Grid (seconds)	Grid Speed-Up Factors
10	1.5	2.5	1.6
100	2.0	16	8
1,000	2.7	164	61
10,000	3.8	2041	537
100,000	4.7	22169	4717
1,000,000	5.2	240,796	46,307

Table

2. Variation in run time with and without regular grids [3].

This would be a required improvement for the number of raindrops that have to be in the scene and make this research possible. Additionally, once photon mapping is implemented as well as photon relaxation, it would be optimal to determine the ideal parameters for achieving an acceptable render time and image quality. In addition, issues not addressed in this paper such as parallelization and distributed methods of implementation would allow for even further speed ups, but are final stage methods that require completed implementation of the tracer. With the information provided earlier, it is the conclusion of the author that the delivered software package provides the foundation for achieving the research goals. As a demonstration of the current capability of the render in path tracing, Figures 6 and 7 are presented with their respective render times:

Figure 6. Path tracing matte material with the following details:
Samples per pixel = 400 Depth = 7 Render Time = 7 minutes 14 seconds

Figure 7. Path tracing matte material with the following details:
Samples per pixel = 4000 Depth = 7 Render time = 2 hours 58 minutes 17 seconds

In addition the following figures are added for dielectric materials using ray tracing, again with render times demonstrating the difference between simple transparency and dielectric materials: Since the publication cannot support full-colour images, the full-colour images of figures can be found at http:
www.dsc.kcl.ac.uk/staff/richard/images

Material	Index of Refraction	Render Time (seconds)
Transparent	1.0 (air)	216
Transparent	1.33 (water)	213
Dielectric	1.0 (air)	253
Dielectric	1.33 (water)	253

Table 3. Variation in render time for Transparent and Dielectric materials

Figure 8: Transparent material with index of refraction = 1.00

Figure 9: Dielectric material with index of refraction = 1.00

Figure 10: Transparent material with index of refraction = 1.33

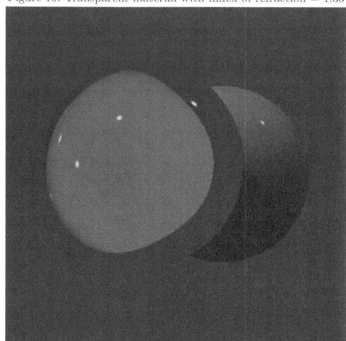

Figure 11: Dielectric material with index of refraction = 1.33

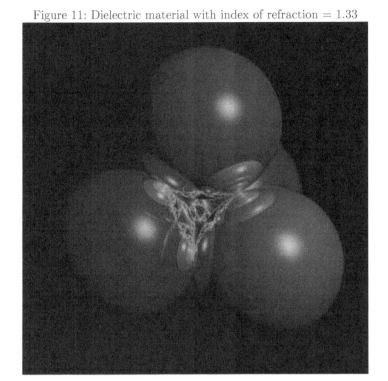

Figure 12: Sierpinksi gasket fractal.

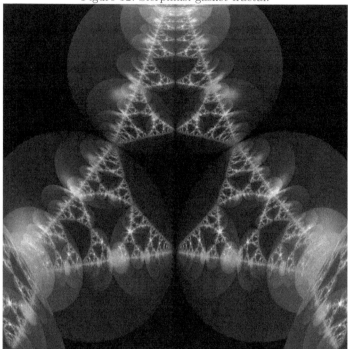

Figure 13: Sierpinksi gasket fractal zoomed in.

5   Summary, Conclusions, and Future Work

In this attempt to produce a renderer that creates vivid, realistic and aesthetically pleasing images, the authors have produced a system which handles the aforementioned dielectric materials, as well as a path tracer which handles matte and reflective materials. Therefore as future work, it is the aim of the authors to proceed to implement a photon mapping solution [6] which can then attempt to follow the methodology outlined for photon relaxation by Spencer [1]. It is the belief of the authors that by using the aforementioned methods to creating the desired imagery is plausible in an efficient time frame with minimal approximation. In addition it represents an exciting implementation of global illumination methods that will mimic dispersion of white light into it's individual components.

6   Bibliography

[1] B. Spencer, "Ben Spencer," 2010. [Online]. Available: http://cs.swan.ac.uk/ cs-benjamin/ [Accessed: April 18, 2010].

[2] Bidirectional reflectance distribution function - Wikipedia, the free encyclopaedia, (n.d.). [Online]. Available: http://en.wikipedia.org/wiki/Optical_phenomenon [Accessed: April 17, 2010]

[3] K. Suffern, *Ray Tracing from the Ground Up*. Wellesley, Massachusetts: A. K. Peters, 2007.

[4] A. Frohn and N.Roth, *Dynamics of Droplets*.1st ed. Stuttgart, Germany: Universität Stuttgart, 1965. [E-book] Available: Google Books.

[5] H X A 7 2 4 1, "< H X A 7 2 4 1 >: Minilight minimal global illumination renderer," 2007. [Online]. Available: http://www.hxa.name/minilight/ [Accessed: April 18, 2010].

[6] H. W. Jensen, *Realistic Image Synthesis via Photon Mapping*, 1st ed. Natick, Massachusetts : A.K. Peters, 2001

Pattern Matching in MIDI Files

Cheng Lu and Prudence W.H. Wong

Department of Computer Science
University of Liverpool
C.Lu2@student.liverpool.ac.uk, pwong@liverpool.ac.uk

1 Introduction

Imagine that we are listening to some songs from the radio. In order to listen to the songs again, we want to find the song but we do not have the name of the song. We only know the melody of a part of the song. How do we search for the song? In this paper, we study the problem of searching a segment of music against a longer piece of music to check if the segment is "similar" to some part of the song or not.

The main problem is to define what it means by "similar". In this paper, we attempt to formalize the problem as some variants of pattern matching problem and adapt existing pattern matching algorithms to solve the problem. We also report on the progress of the implementation of a software for doing this.

Music can be stored in different format. For the sake of simplicity, we focus on the MIDI files [5], which provide a common file format used by most musical software and hardware devices to store song information including the title, track names, and most importantly what instruments are used and the sequence of musical events, such as notes and instrument control information needed to play back the song.

The problem we study here is a pattern matching problem. We are given a short piece of song fragment (c.f. pattern in the context of pattern matching) and a complete song (c.f. text). The objective is to determine if the pattern appears in the text with some minor modifications. Minor modifications may include modified tune or speed (formal definition will be given in Section 3). This paper discusses the progress of the work to perform pattern matching in MIDI files.

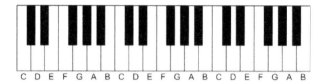

Fig. 1. Musical notes arranged on a piano.

2 Preliminaries

2.1 Musical notations and MIDI files

Notes and scales. A piece of music / song can be described as a sequence of musical notes which follow rhythmic patterns and structure. One of the most important music notations is the scale. Music theory generally divides the notes into a series of twelve notes. The series of notes is usually referred to as a *scale*. The twelve notes include an octave of seven distinct notes (plus an eighth which duplicate the first one but an octave higher). These notes correspond to the syllables "Do, Re, Mi, Fa, So, La, Ti, (Do)". Some notes may also be sharp (indicated by a # character), or flat (indicated by ♭). This makes another five additional notes to form a total of twelve. The notes are written from A to G. For example, for C major, the correspondence of note and syllables are as follows.

C	C#/D♭	D	D#/E♭	E	F	F#/G♭	G	G#/A♭	A	A#/B♭	B	C
Do		Re		Mi	Fa		So		La		Ti	Do

Note that one note can be considered as sharp or flat, e.g., C# and D♭ is the same note. Figure 1 shows the notes arranged on a piano. A scale is named in terms of the starting note of the scale. For example, a C major starts with the note C. Figure 2 shows the list of twelve major scales.

A piece of music can be written in different musical scales but may still sound similar. For example, C in C major sounds as 'Do' while G in G major also sounds as 'Do'. When we match two pieces of music, the letters of the notes can be very different but they may still sound similar. For example, the sequence of notes CDEFG in C

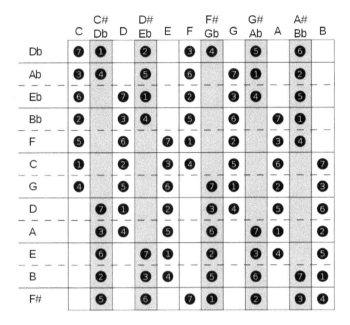

Fig. 2. Musical notes arranged on a piano.

major sounds similar as GABCD in G major as both of them sound as 'Do, Re, Mi, Fa, So'.

MIDI file and timing. In a MIDI file, each of the notes (of different octaves) is encoded by integers. For example, C in the fourth octave C4, usually referred as the middle C, is encoded as 60; C#4 as 61, D4 as 62, D#4 as 63, and so on. As shown later, the matching will be done by comparing the encoded integers of the notes.

Apart from the note, another important concept is the time at which the note is sounded. In a MIDI file, a note is associated with two integers indicating the starting (note-on) and ending (note-off) time of the note. Two pieces of music may have different note-on and note-off time for each note but if the relative duration preserves, they may sound similar as well. As a result, the matching also has to take into account the duration of the notes.

75

2.2 Matching algorithms

String matching has been a very well studied problem. In this section, we discuss some well known matching algorithms. The discussion is not meant to be exhaustive. The naive string matching algorithm checks every position i in the text to determine if the pattern matches the substring of the text starting from position i. This algorithms takes $O(nm)$ time where n is the length of the text and m is the length of the pattern.

The Knuth-Morris-Pratt algorithm [1] presented a linear time algorithm. The KMP algorithm makes use of an auxiliary prefix function that is precomputed by comparing the pattern against itself. For a pattern $P[1..m]$, the prefix function $\pi : \{1, 2, \cdots, m\} \rightarrow \{0, 1, ..., m - 1\}$ is defined such that $\pi(q)$ is the length of the longest prefix of P that is a proper suffix of $P[1..q]$. With this prefix function, when the matching of the pattern against the text is failed at a certain position $P[q]$, instead of shifting one position for the next test, we can shift by $\pi(q)$. This reduces the time complexity to $O(n + m)$. Other well-known matching algorithms include the Rabin-Karp algorithm [2] and the Boyer-Moore algorithm [3].

3 The problem and solution

3.1 The problem

In this section, we formally define the problem. A MIDI file can be considered as sequence of n musical notes, denoted as $T = \{t_1, t_2, t_3, \cdots, t_n\}$. Each note t_i is a triple $\{key_i, \alpha_i, \beta_i\}$, where key_i is the note encoded as integer, α_i and β_i are the time at the which the note is on and off, respectively. Similarly, we denote a pattern as $P = \{p_1, p_2, \cdots, p_m\}$. The pattern P is said to be *key-similar* to the text T if there exists a position i and an integer offest $\epsilon \in Z$ such that $key(t_{i+j-1}) = key(p_j) + \epsilon$ for all $1 \le j \le m$.

For example, if the keys of the text are $\cdots$, 60 (C), 64 (E), 60 (C), $\cdots$ and those for the pattern are 67 (G), 71 (B), 67 (G), then the pattern is key-similar to the text with an offset 7.

As we mentioned before, two pieces of music may have exactly the same notes but are played at different speed and sound similar. This happens when the relative duration of each note is the same.

The definition is slightly more complicated. We say that a pattern P is *time-similar* to the text T if there exists a position i and an offset $\epsilon \in R$ such that

1. $\beta(t_{i+j-1}) - \alpha(t_{i+j-1}) = \epsilon * (\beta(p_j) - \alpha(p_j))$, for all $1 \leq j \leq m$, and
2. $\alpha(t_{i+j}) - \alpha(t_{i+j-1}) = \epsilon * (\alpha(p_{j+1}) - \alpha(p_j))$, for all $1 \leq j < m$.

For example, if the note-on and note-off tuples of the text are $\cdots$, $(1, 3)$, $(2, 3)$, $(3, 5)$, $(4, 5)$, $\cdots$ and those of the pattern are $(1, 5)$, $(3, 5)$, $(5, 9)$, $(7, 9)$, then the pattern is time-similar to the text.

Given a text, the problem is to determine if a pattern is key-similar and/or time-similar to the text.

3.2 Algorithmic solution

To determine if a pattern is key-similar to a text, we can modify the naive string matching algorithm slightly (see Algorithm 1). When we match the pattern against the i-th position of the text, we first compute the offset between $P[1]$ and $T[i]$ and then check that every pair of values followed also differ by this offset.

Algorithm 1 Algorithm to check key-similarity of pattern P against text T.

---

for $i = 1$ to $n - m$ do
    $\epsilon = key(P[1]) - key(T[i])$
    $j = 2$
    while $j \leq m$ and $key(P[j]) - key(T[i+j-1]) == \epsilon$ do
        $j = j + 1$
    if $j == m$ then
        report "Match!"

As for the time-similarity, we also modify the naive algorithm as in Algorithm 2. The time complexity of the algorithm is $O(nm)$ for both Algorithms 1 and 2.

3.3 Software

A software has been implemented to allow user to specify a MIDI file as text and another MIDI file as pattern, and check key- and time-similarity. Figure 3 shows a simple interface of the input and

Algorithm 2 Algorithm to check time-similarity of pattern P against text T.

---

define $d(s) = \beta(s) - \alpha(s)$
for $i = 1$ to $n - m$ do
    $\epsilon = d(P[1])/d(T[i])$
    $j = 2$
    while $j \leq m$ and $d(P[j])/d(T[i+j-1]) == \epsilon$
        and $(\alpha(P[j]) - \alpha(P[j-1]))/(\alpha(T[i+j]/\alpha(T[i+j-1)) == \epsilon$ do
        $j = j + 1$
    if $j == m$ then
        report "Match!"

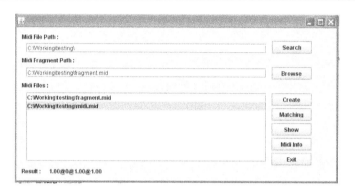

Fig. 3. A simple interface to select MIDI file and midi fragment.

Figure 4 shows the matching result. Another interface has also been implemented to allow user to input a MIDI file

4 Concluding remarks

This paper describes the problem of matching two pieces of music to determine whether they are similar in terms of tones and speed. The next step is to improve the efficiency of the matching algorithms. The idea of the KMP algorithm may not be used directly since when a pattern is compared against itself, every character can be a prefix of each other with some offset.

An immediate extension of the work is to experiment on other matching algorithms and compare their performance. At the moment, the software focuses on a single channel. An interesting direc-

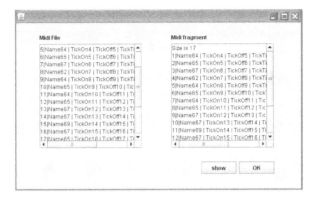

Fig. 4. The matching result using the naive algorithm that reports key-similarity.

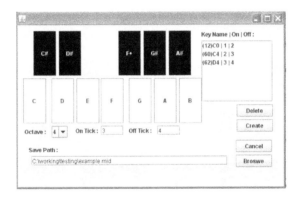

Fig. 5. A simple interface to create a MIDI file.

tion would be to consider multiple channels as a whole. There is also other work that attempts to first extract the melody of the music and only compare those parts that are more likely to be perceived as the melody of the piece of music. Uitdenbogerd and Zobel [4] gave some comparison of different techniques to extract the melody.

References

1. D. Knuth, J. H. Morris and V. Pratt. Fast pattern matching in strings. SIAM Journal on Computing, 6(2):323–350, 1977.
2. R. Karp and M. Rabin. Efficient randomized pattern-matching algorithms. IBM Journal of Research and Development, 31(2):249–260, 1987.

3. R.S. Boyer and J.S. Moore. A fast string searching algorithm. Communications of the Association for Computing Machinery, 20(10):762-772, 1977.

4. A. Uitdenbogerd and J. Zobel. Melodic matching techniques for large music databases. Proceedings of the seventh ACM international conference on Multimedia, 57-66, 1999.

5. Paul White. Basic MIDI. Sanctuary Publishing Ltd. 2000.

Experimental Analysis of Speed Scaling Algorithms

Philip Livesey and Prudence W.H. Wong

Department of Computer Science
University of Liverpool
P.Livesey@student.liverpool.ac.uk, pwong@liverpool.ac.uk

1   Introduction

Energy usage has become a major issue in the design of microprocessors, especially for battery-operated devices. Modern processors support dynamic speed scaling to reduce energy usage. Recently there is a lot of research on online job scheduling taking speed scaling and energy usage into consideration (see [6] for a survey). The challenge arises from the conflicting objectives of providing good quality of service and conserving energy. Most results are based on a speed scaling model in which a processor, when running at speed s, consumes energy at the rate of s^α, where α is typically 2 [11] or 3 (the cube-root rule [4]).

A commonly used QoS measure for job scheduling is total flow time. The flow time of a job is the time from the job arrives until it is completed. In the online setting, jobs with arbitrary work requirements (or sizes) arrive at unpredictable times. They are to be run on a processor which allows preemption without penalty. Albers and Fujiwara [1] initiated the study of minimizing a linear combination of total flow and total energy. From an economic viewpoint, both flow and energy can be compared with respect to their monetary value, and it can be assumed that users are willing to pay a certain (say, ρ) units of energy to reduce one unit of flow time. Then, one would like to minimize the total flow plus the total energy weighted with ρ. By changing the units of time and energy, one can further assume that $\rho = 1$ [10].

At any time, an online scheduling algorithm has to determine which job to run and at what speed this job runs. To minimize flow

	$\alpha = 2$	$\alpha = 3$
BPS	5.236 [3]	7.940 [3]
AJC	**2.667** [10]	**3.252** [10]

Table 1. Competitive ratio of BPS and AJC when $\alpha = 2$ and 3.

time only, SRPT (shortest remaining processing time) is an optimal strategy. Bansal, Pruhs and Stein [3] has proposed to scale the speed as a function of unfinished work and is $O((\frac{\alpha}{\ln \alpha})^2)$-competitive for minimizing flow plus energy Later Lam et al. [10] proposed to scale the speed as a function of the number of unfinished jobs. The function, called AJC (active job count), is $O(\frac{\alpha}{\ln \alpha})$-competitive. Figure 1 shows the competitive ratio of BPS and AJC when $\alpha = 2$ and 3.

In this paper, we study how the performance changes as a function of the number of unfinished jobs. We experiment different speed functions and compare them against each other and with a fixed speed function.

2   Model and algorithms

Consider a job set to be scheduled on a processor whose speed can vary. When the processor runs at speed s, the processor processes s units of work and consumes s^α units of energy in each unit of time, where $\alpha > 1$. Preemption is allowed and a preempted job can be resumed at the point of preemption. Each job J_i comes with an arbitrary arrival time a_i and size p_i. If the arrival time of all jobs is the same, we call the jobs *batched jobs*.

Consider a particular time t in a schedule. For any job J_i, let q_i denote its remaining work at time t. We say that J_i is active if $r_i \leq t$ and $q_i > 0$. The *flow time* F_i of J_i is the time elapsed since it arrives until it is completed. The *total flow time* F is defined as the sum of flow time of all jobs, i.e., $\sum_i F_i$. Note that $F = \int_0^\infty n(t)\mathrm{d}t$, where $n(t)$ denotes the number of active jobs at time t. Our aim is to schedule all the jobs to completion so as to minimize the total flow time plus energy.

An online algorithm has to make decision as the jobs arrive without future information. We measure the performance of an online algorithm by competitive analysis. An algorithm is said to be c-competitive if its flow time plus energy is at most c times that of the optimal algorithm.

We now describe the two algorithms BPS and AJC. At any time t, let $q(t)$ be the total amount of remaining work of all active jobs. BPS selects the job with the smallest size (SJF) and runs it at the speed $q(t)^{1/\alpha}$. AJC selects the jobs with the smallest remaining work (SRPT) and runs it at the speed $n(t)^{1/\alpha}$, where $n(t)$ is the number of active jobs at time t.

3 Experiments

Generating random job sets. We generate various job sets to test different speed functions. There are two types of job sets depending on the number of jobs. We take 100 jobs and 800 jobs as the number of jobs to represent small and large job sets, respectively.

The job attributes including arrival time and job size are generated randomly. We distinguish the batch job sets and random arrival job sets. For batch job sets, all the jobs arrive at time 0 and the only difference is the size of the jobs. For random arrival job sets, the arrival time of job $a(j)$ is set to be $a(j-1) + r$, where r is random number between 0 and d and d is a number indicating whether the job set is dense or sparse. We set $d = 2$ for densely arrived jobs and $d = 10$ for sparsely arrived jobs. The job size is also generated randomly between 1 and 100 units. For each setting of the job set we considered, we generate 20 instances and take the average over the 20 instances.

Determining speed scaling function. As mentioned before, the speed function AJC depends on the number of active jobs. Precisely, AJC sets the speed to be $n^{1/\alpha}$, where n is the number of active jobs. We first carry out experiments to test if this is a reasonable speed function to be used. For this, we tried various speed function including n, $n^{9/10}$, $n^{4/5}$, $n^{1/2}$, $n^{1/3}$, $n^{1/5}$, and $n^{0.1}$. Figures 1 and 2 show the result when $\alpha = 2$. Both show that the flow time plus energy decreases as the power decreases and stabilizes at about the point $n^{1/2}$, indicating that $n^{1/\alpha}$ could be a reasonable speed function to use. One might argue that we could have chosen a lower power to decrease the total flow time plus energy further, but then this would increase the flow time significantly.

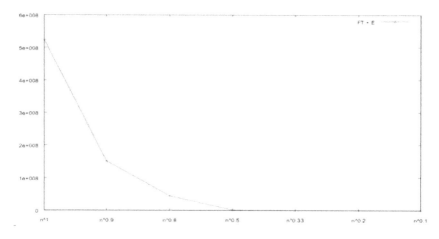

Fig. 1. Flow time plus energy versus different speed functions for $\alpha = 2$ and 100 jobs in the job set.

Dynamic speed function versus fixed speed function. We now compare the performance of using dynamic speed function and fixed speed function. For each scenario we test, we measure the ratio of the performance of using fixed speed function versus the speed function $n^{1/\alpha}$. We test tried different fixed speed values to find one that gives similar flow time as the speed function $n^{1/\alpha}$. For example, for $\alpha = 2$ and 100 jobs in the job set, we find that using a fixed speed of 6.2 gives a similar flow time as the function $n^{1/\alpha}$. We then compare the energy used between these two functions. We find that the energy used and flow time plus energy of the fixed speed function is always more than the dynamic speed function. Figure 3 shows that for $\alpha = 2$ and 100 job in the job set, the energy of using fixed speed function is about 1.15 times using dynamic speed function. Similar result is obtained when $\alpha = 3$ with the ratio around 1.10 (see Figure 4).

When we test this on a larger job set with 800 jobs, the fixed speed giving similar flow time as the dynamic speed function is found to be 6.85. Using this fixed speed, we obtain similar results that the

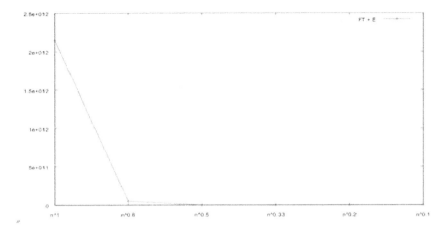

Fig. 2. Flow time plus energy versus different speed functions for $\alpha = 2$ and 800 jobs in the job set.

energy used is about 1.15 to 1.2 times that used with dynamic speed function (see Figures 5 and 6. As can be seen in these graphs, in the majority of cases the dynamic speed algorithm was slightly faster to finish than the constant speed algorithm, and yet it still remains more efficient in terms of energy by quite a large margin. Another observation is that the dynamic speed algorithm seems to get better the more jobs we have. The ratio of flow time plus energy in the 800 job case is about 1.15, whereas in the 100 job situation it is around 1.10.

We further consider densely arrived jobs where the average inter-arrival time is 2 time units. Figures 7 and 8 shows that for such arrival pattern, the dynamic speed algorithm is still superior to the constant speed algorithm.

4 Concluding remarks

To conclude, we have carried out experiments to compare the performance of different speed functions. The first observation is that if we vary the speed, the speed function $n^{1/\alpha}$ is a good choice. The second observation is that if we identify a fixed speed such that the flow time used is similar to the flow time used when using $n^{1/\alpha}$, the

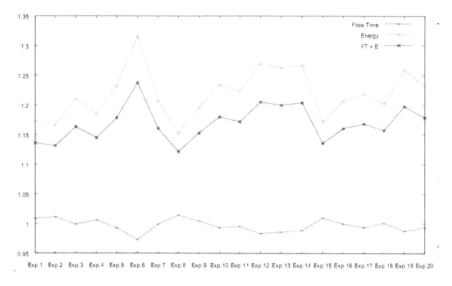

Fig. 3. Ratio of fixed speed of 6.2 versus speed $n^{1/\alpha}$ for $\alpha = 2$ and 100 batch jobs in the job set.

dynamic speed function always gives smaller energy and flow time plus energy.

We also identify a number of possible future directions.

Other energy-flow scheduling algorithms. Recently, another algorithm [2] has been proposed to improve the competitive ratio to $3 + \epsilon$ regardless of the value of α. It is desirable to carry out experiments on this algorithm as well.

LRPT vs SRPT. SRPT has been proved to be optimal in flow time if the speed is fixed. It is unclear whether this job selection strategy is also the best when the speed is dynamic. At first glance, LRPT (longest remaining processing time) running the job with longest remaining processing time may lead to accumulation of jobs but on the other hand, this will likely increase the speed leading to smaller flow time. One may study the use of LRPT together with some speed function and see if any such combination may give better result.

Multiprocessor scheduling. Our experiments focus on a single processor. An interesting direction is to carry out experiments on

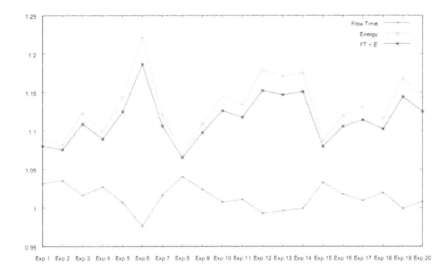

Fig. 4. Ratio of fixed speed of 3.46 versus speed $n^{1/\alpha}$ for $\alpha = 3$ and 100 batch jobs in the job set.

multiprocessors. There is some theoretical work [5, 8, 9] on this aspect and so any experimental work would supplement the theoretical study.

Dynamic speed scaling with sleep states. The current model we study assumes that when the speed is zero, the energy consumption is zero. However, in reality, there is likely some leakage. A more realistic model would be that the power is $s^\alpha + \sigma$, where σ is static energy required even when the speed is zero. To have zero power, the processor enters a sleep state but wake-up to an awake state requires paying ω units of energy. This model has been studied [7]. It would be desirable to experiment on the algorithm proposed.

References

1. S. Albers and H. Fujiwara. Energy-efficient algorithms for flow time minimization. *ACM Transactions on Algorithms*, 3(4):49, 2007.
2. N. Bansal, H. L. Chan, and K. Pruhs. Speed scaling with an arbitrary power function. In *Proceedings of ACM-SIAM Symposium on Discrete Algorithms (SODA)*, pages 693–701, 2009.

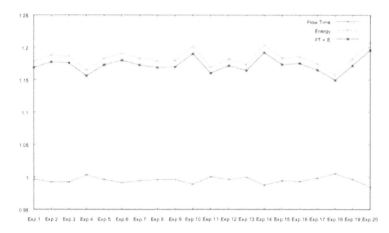

Fig. 5. Ratio of fixed speed of 6.2 versus speed $n^{1/\alpha}$ for $\alpha = 2$ and 800 batch jobs in the job set.

3. N. Bansal, K. Pruhs, and C. Stein. Speed scaling for weighted flow time. In *Proceedings of ACM-SIAM Symposium on Discrete Algorithms (SODA)*, pages 805–813, 2007.
4. D. M. Brooks, P. Bose, S. E. Schuster, H. Jacobson, P. N. Kudva, A. Buyukto-sunoglu, J. D. Wellman, V. Zyuban, M. Gupta, and P. W. Cook. Power-aware microarchitecture: Design and modeling challenges for next-generation micropro-cessors. *IEEE Micro*, 20(6):26–44, 2000.
5. G. Greiner, T. Nonner, and A. Souza. The bell is ringing in speed-scaled multipro-cessor scheduling. In *Proceedings of ACM Symposium on Parallelism in Algorithms and Architectures (SPAA)*, pages 11–18, 2009.
6. S. Irani and K. Pruhs. Algorithmic problems in power management. *ACM SIGACT News*, 32(2):63–76, 2005.
7. T. W. Lam, L. K. Lee, H. F. Ting, I. K. K. To, and P. W. H. Wong. Sleep with guilt and work faster to minimize flow plus energy. In *Proceedings of International Colloquium on Automata, Languages and Programming (ICALP)*, pages 665–676, 2009.
8. T. W. Lam, L. K. Lee, I. K. K. To, and P. W. H. Wong. Competitive non-migratory scheduling for flow time and energy. In *Proceedings of ACM Symposium on Parallelism in Algorithms and Architectures (SPAA)*, pages 256–264, 2008.
9. T. W. Lam, L. K. Lee, I. K. K. To, and P. W. H. Wong. Non-migratory multi-processor scheduling for response time and energy. *IEEE Transactions on Parallel and Distributed Systems*, 19(11):1527–1539, 2008.
10. T. W. Lam, L. K. Lee, I. K. K. To, and P. W. H. Wong. Speed scaling functions for flow time scheduling based on active job count. In *Proceedings of European Symposium on Algorithms (ESA)*, pages 647–659, 2008.
11. T. Mudge. Power: A first-class architectural design constraint. *Computer*, 34(4):52–58, 2001.

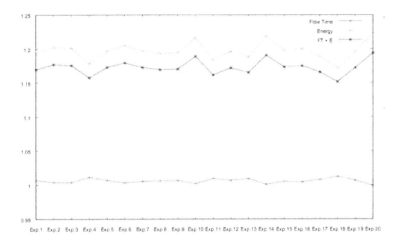

Fig. 6. Ratio of fixed speed of 3.46 versus speed $n^{1/\alpha}$ for $\alpha = 3$ and 800 batch jobs in the job set.

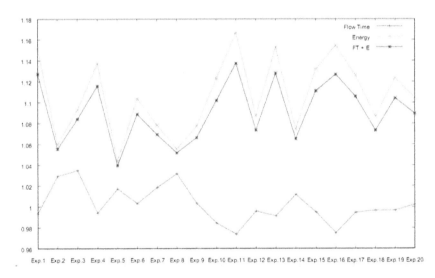

Fig. 7. Ratio of fixed speed of 5.8 versus speed $n^{1/\alpha}$ for $\alpha = 2$ and 100 densely arrived jobs in the job set.

89

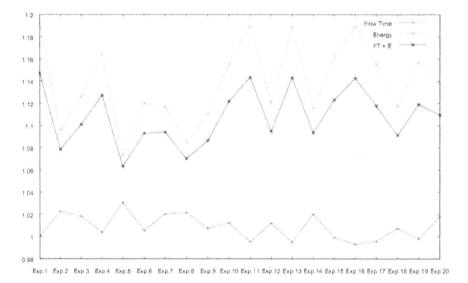

Fig. 8. Ratio of fixed speed of 3.3 versus speed $n^{1/\alpha}$ for $\alpha = 3$ and 100 densely arrived jobs in the job set.

www.ingramcontent.com/pod-product-compliance
Lightning Source LLC
LaVergne TN
LVHW012332060326

832902LV00011B/1859